Preparing Effective Teachers of Reading

PETER LANG
New York • Washington, D.C./Baltimore • Bern
Frankfurt am Main • Berlin • Brussels • Vienna • Oxford

Preparing Effective Teachers of Reading

Putting Research Findings to Work for Student Learning

Boyce C. Williams, EDITOR

PETER LANG
New York • Washington, D.C./Baltimore • Bern
Frankfurt am Main • Berlin • Brussels • Vienna • Oxford

Library of Congress Cataloging-in-Publication Data

Preparing effective teachers of reading: putting research findings
to work for student learning / [edited by] Boyce C. Williams.
p. cm.
Includes bibliographical references.
1. Reading teachers—Training of. 2. Effective teaching.
I. Williams, Boyce C. (Boyce Courtney)
LB2844.1.R4P737   428.4'071—dc22   2007045053
ISBN 978-1-4331-0132-8 (hardcover)
ISBN 978-1-4331-0131-1 (paperback)

Bibliographic information published by **Die Deutsche Bibliothek**.
Die Deutsche Bibliothek lists this publication in the "Deutsche
Nationalbibliografie"; detailed bibliographic data is available
on the Internet at http://dnb.ddb.de/.

The Standard of Excellence
in Teacher Preparation

Cover image: young readers in the Even Start Family Literacy Program
benefiting from tutoring provided by pre-service teachers
from Albany State University, a NCATE/RFTEN partner institution
Cover design by Clear Point Designs

The paper in this book meets the guidelines for permanence and durability
of the Committee on Production Guidelines for Book Longevity
of the Council of Library Resources.

"You Can't Read to Learn until You First Learn to Read"

This eloquent quotation, distributed to those attending the 2002 White House Initiative on Historically Black Colleges and Universities Conference, gave rise to the Reading First Teacher Education Network (RFTEN) project. This book is dedicated to the preeminent U.S. Secretary of Education (2000–2004), the Honorable Roderick R. Paige. Dr. Paige was the seventh U.S. Secretary of Education and the first to serve in the twenty-first century; he made history when he became the first African American Secretary of Education.

Contents

Preface

Reading First Teacher Education Network (RFTEN) is the National Council for Accreditation of Teacher Education's (NCATE's) largest developmental effort to date in terms of scope and scale. We decided in 2003 to launch the RFTEN project and engage a selected group of our NCATE institutions because we were concerned that so many of the nation's teachers were not being adequately prepared to teach all youngsters. The RFTEN project and scientifically based reading research (SBRR) represented solutions to a terrible problem in American education.

The RFTEN project enabled NCATE to consider the first coherent and comprehensive research-based approach to teaching what is, after all, the most fundamental of subjects, reading. Periodically, NCATE revises its standards on the basis of new knowledge and new experience. Over the course of the RFTEN project, consensus has grown about this approach being one strategy for working with youngsters who have difficulty learning how to read.

Today, NCATE and its partner organizations, the International Reading Association and the Association for Childhood Education International—two organizations with which we work on elementary standards—are proposing that the SBRR practices used in RFTEN become even more central to the preparation of elementary school teachers. The RFTEN project has been a turning point, not only for the institutions directly involved in the project but also for the larger educational community.

Arthur E. Wise

NCATE/RFTEN Project Abstract

Preparing Highly Qualified Teachers to Leave No Child Behind

The mission of No Child Left Behind is to work with schools, communities, colleges and the private sector to meet the needs of all children. The Children's Defense Fund Action Council in its 2005 *State of America's Children: Action Guide* states that: "We must build a nation fit for all children regardless of the political and economic weather. Don't be afraid to stand up for principles that matter; set goals, develop an action plan for achieving them and keep moving until we reach them. Recognize and use your power to make a difference for others and finally let's believe we can make a difference, then do it for children."

The Reading First Education Network (RFTEN) project believed it could make a difference. Through its partnerships with the National Institute for Child Health and Development (NICHD) and the Vaughn Gross Center for Reading and Language Arts (VGCRLA) it was able to address issues of "literacy" that plagued America's children. RFTEN believed that through a concerted strategic partnership it could merge the science, research and practice to prepare teachers (new and practicing) to teach reading throughout the curriculum for all children. The National Council for Accreditation of Teacher Education (NCATE) chose, through RFTEN, to emphasize reading using its content area standards to prepare teachers and to change the way faculty taught reading as a means to increase student achievement.

Because parents cannot teach what they have not been taught it was important that through this project parents were supported in developing networks and workshops to help with reading and literacy development.

The purpose of the project was to enhance the implementation of scientifically based reading research at Historically Black Colleges and Universities (HBCUs), Hispanic Serving Institutions (HSIs), and Tribal Colleges by:

1. engaging college and university presidents and deans in realigning their reading instruction with effective research-based practices in reading; and
2. engaging professors who prepare teachers in a series of focused, collaborative meetings that provide access to guides, materials, and training in scientifically based research in reading to be incorporated into their instruction.

At the end of the project, as outlined in the book, teacher education faculty at minority-serving institutions were able to demonstrate that they knew relevant scientifically-based research on the teaching of reading and how to apply this research in the classroom to help teacher candidates teach reading to Pre-K–12 students to help them make solid achievement gains in reading.

In the first and second year, NCATE worked jointly with the University of Texas Center for Reading and Language Arts Higher Education Collaborative (UTCRLA/HEC), and NICHD on this project. NCATE previously operated a Historically Black College and University Technical Support Network that strengthened the overall teacher preparation programs at HBCUs. The UTCRLA/HEC currently conducts training in scientifically-based reading research and instruction to faculty at higher education institutions. NICHD is considered one of the leading research centers for reading instruction.

The UTCRLA/HEC, now (VGCRLA) convened leading researchers who operated an intensive training program for faculty from minority-serving institutions and for consultants who aided those institutions during the project. CRLA/HEC and NICHD personnel committed to serving as lead trainers on this project. Reading consultants were assigned to each participating institution and will aid the institutions in determining where the curriculum needs change and what additional resources the institutions need to deliver the training to faculty and candidates.

NCATE contracted with institutions to help build capacity. NCATE collaborated with deans and presidents in the institutions to ensure that scientifically-based reading research and instruction become the basis for change in the preparation of new teachers. This administrative role included overseeing the use of the results of the needs assessment in reconstruction of curricula, collaborating with deans to ensure the instruction reflected faculty training in SBRR (Scientifically Based Reading Research) and that teacher candidates' acquisition of scientifically-based reading research was evident in their practicum experiences. NCATE's role in the reading initiative, through its consultants, assured that deans:

1. collaborate with professors to ensure that ongoing dialogue occurs with public school faculty regarding elementary students' reading skills and the assessment of those skills;
2. develop a plan for extending the SBRR training to other faculty within the SOE (School of Education)who are responsible for the preparation of pre-service teachers;
3. maintain documentation of teacher candidate licensure outcomes; and
4. establish a professional learning community, including an on-line community of practice in which faculty regularly dialogue about adjustments to their instruction and materials to enhance the implementation of the scientifically-based reading research. In addition, NCATE will work with consultants to assure that presidents receive an overview of scientifically-based reading research, dialogue with deans regarding the results of needs assessment and implications for reforming the preparation of teacher candidates, and monitor the alignment of teacher preparation course curricula with effective research-based practices in reading. Once the institutions are working on their program changes, the University of Texas CRLA/HEC and NCATE will hold workshops for the 25 institutions that attended the training.

NCATE also worked with testing companies and states on ways to assess what candidates know about scientifically-based reading instruction. In year three, we evaluated the results of the project by evaluating changes in the institutions' reading instruction and preparation of teacher candidates. Information was gathered from teacher candidates who were student teaching to determine how the curriculum materials and approaches were being used. Information was also provided by the institutions on licensure exam accomplishments of candidates, resulting in the publication by Diana W. Rigden, Ph.D., titled *Licensure Alignment with the Essential Components of Effective Reading Instruction* in August 2006. NCATE published project outcomes in print, on the web, and in newsletters and monographs; produced a video; offered professional development and teaching tools on a specially designed RFTEN website; and presented at over fifty conferences and meetings.

Boyce C. Williams

Prelude

"The test of our progress is not whether we add more to the abundance of those who have much; it is whether we provide enough for those who have too little."

PRESIDENT FRANKLIN D. ROOSEVELT

In December 2000, George W. Bush was effectively named the 43rd president of the United States as a result of the Supreme Court ruling on electoral balloting, recounts, and hanging chads. At the top of his list of legislative priorities was federal legislation to redesign, overhaul, and refocus the Elementary and Secondary Education Act (ESEA) that was pending reauthorization. Just three days after his inauguration, President Bush announced the cornerstone legislation of his administration—the No Child Left Behind Act of 2001 (NCLB). President Bush touted NCLB as an educational reform framework that would supply underachieving American children with a quality education.

The No Child Left Behind Act describes the ways in which America's elementary and secondary schools are to be held accountable for their underachieving students as well as the ways in which they might improve. The NCLB Act reauthorizes the ESEA and incorporates four broad principles and strategies. First, NCLB increases accountability for states, school districts, and schools. States are required to implement statewide accountability systems that challenge state standards for reading and mathematics in public schools. In addition, these systems require annual testing for all students in grades 3–8 and annual statewide goals to ensure all groups of students reach a designated proficiency level within twelve years. States are required to report assessment results and relative state objectives by poverty, race, ethnicity, disability, and limited English proficiency to ensure that no group is underachieving or "left behind." School districts and schools that fail to make adequate yearly progress (AYP) toward statewide proficiency goals will be subject to improvement, corrective action, and restructuring measures aimed at restoring them to state compliance. Schools that meet or exceed AYP objectives or close achievement gaps will be eligible for state academic achievement awards.

Second, NCLB offers greater choice for parents and students, particularly those attending low-performing schools. The NCLB Act increases the schooling options for students attending Title I schools that fail to meet state standards. Local educational agencies (LEAs) are required to give students the opportunity to attend a better public or public charter school if the school in which the student is enrolled is identified for improvement, corrective action, or restructuring. The district is required to provide transportation to the new school and designate 5 percent of Title I funding for this purpose (if needed). Title I funds may also be used to supplement educational services from selected public or private sector providers for students attending persistently failing schools. Providers must meet state standards and offer services tailored to help participating students meet challenging state academic standards. School districts are also required to earmark 20 percent of their Title I allocations for school choice and supplemental educational services that assist LEAs to offer meaningful choices to eligible students. Low-performing schools will receive a substantial incentive to improve. Schools that underperform will be restructured if they do not make adequate yearly progress for five years.

Third, NCLB provides more flexibility for states and local educational agencies in the use of federal education dollars. States and LEAs are authorized to transfer up to 50 percent between state grant programs or to Title I. The State Flexibility Demonstration Program permits as many as seven states to consolidate funding from the state share and nearly all federal state grants. Additional flexibility is provided in the spending of Title V (innovation) funds. Participating states enter five-year performance agreements with the secretary of education that consolidated funds may be used for any educational purpose authorized under the ESEA. States also enter ten-year local performance agreements with LEAs. LEAs receive flexibility under the separate Local Flexibility Demonstration Program, which adds eighty LEAs to the existing seventy under the State Flexibility Demonstration Program. The following funds may be consolidated under this program: Teacher Quality State Grants, Educational Technology State Grants, Innovative Programs, and Safe and Drug-Free Schools programs. Participating LEAs would enter into performance agreements with the secretary of education and may use the consolidated funds for any ESEA-authorized purpose.

Finally, NCLB anchors a stronger emphasis on reading, especially for the nation's youngest children. The NCLB Act fully implements the president's Reading First initiative. Reading First was established to significantly increase the federal investment in scientifically-based reading instruction programs in primary grades. The major rationale of this initiative is to avoid misidentifying children as special education students if these students have received inappropriate reading instruction during their early schooling. Local Reading First grant recipients will administer screening and diagnostic assessments to determine at-risk or reading-deficient students in grades K–3. Professional development is provided for K–3 teachers in the essential components of reading instruction. The Reading First program supported early language, literacy, and pre-reading development of preschool-age children, particularly those from low-income families. Recipients will use research-based instructional strategies and professional development to help young students attain fundamental knowledge and skills for optimal reading development.

It is this fourth plank of NCLB that has critical import for the scholars of this book—reading readiness, reading ability, and reading comprehension for the nation's youth. Under the appropriations for the NCLB Act, the U.S. government focused unprecedented resources (more than $1 billion per year for a period of six years) on reading instruction in high-poverty, low-performing schools. Former U.S. Secretary of Education Roderick Paige often proclaimed, "You can't read to learn until you first learn to read."

M. Christopher Brown II

What Teachers Must Know and Be Able to Do

The Politics of Pedagogy and the Power of Preparation

Reading First + Teacher Education = RFTEN

This book, details the valiant efforts of a group of educators to merge the federal mandate with the preparation of professional educators to improve the outcomes of schooling for the nation's children. RFTEN engaged professors responsible for teacher preparation and candidate licensure in a series of collaborative seminars designed to enhance their knowledge of scientifically based reading strategies, which are incorporated into their curriculum and instructional practices. A unique aspect of RFTEN was its provision of targeted professional development in reading for faculty from more than one hundred minority-serving institutions and/or pipeline programs for high-need, urban, and hard-to-staff school systems. The aim was to promote, improve, and facilitate scientifically based reading strategies among the teachers to enhance the likelihood of *all* children achieving adequate yearly progress.

As chronicled here, RFTEN asserted that preparing teachers to provide high-quality reading instruction is a career-long process. During the initial preparation period at the university, teacher candidates become knowledgeable about research theory regarding how individuals learn to read; however, the complex process of teaching reading is more active than passive (Lefever-Davis, 2002). Scientific evidence details the role of decoding alphabetic symbols and drawing upon prior linguistic experiences to effectuate reading ability. As such, teachers must know that reading is a multidimensional act. Furthermore, teachers must be able to show proficiency in phonemic awareness, decoding, and comprehension. Teachers must plan and present lessons that address the needs of each student by using appropriate instructional approaches and materials which give respect to the differing realities that each student brings to the classroom (Commeyras & DeGroff, 1998; Grant & Wong, 2003). RFTEN taught all of the above.

Preparing beginning teachers in the United States to teach reading well is a national priority. There is, however, great variability in the competence of beginning teachers as they emerge from their teacher preparation programs. Some beginning teachers have as many as twenty-four semester hours of work related to reading instruction, whereas others have as few as three semester hours (Hoffman & Pearson, 2000; Cantrell, 2002; Maloch, Fine, & Flint, 2002/2003). It is essential that we have better-prepared teachers who are competent to teach reading if national and state goals for closing the reading achievement gap (i.e., differences in reading achievement between African American, Hispanic, and Native American students and their white counterparts) are to be realized. This book gives empirical guidance on how to teach reading in a manner that evinces the greatest ambition for all children.

The Importance of Pedagogical Preparation

The national inactivity regarding curricular pedagogy and the moratorium on vilification of teachers have both been lifted (Cuban, 1984, 1990; Cochran-Smith & Lytle, 2001). The national corpus has entered the classroom with reckless abandon. To be fair, some of the recent scrutiny is warranted. Indeed, despite some genuinely valiant, even heroic, efforts, American education continues to sink into a bog where accreditation is mistaken for competency. Inadequate babysitting is often mistaken for teaching. Moreover, many of our classrooms have come to be considered dumping grounds for the underprepared and uninterested. Conversely, many of the recently prescribed panaceas for the academic diagnosis are practices that many educators are already employing in their pedagogical practice.

Many of the difficult realities in school settings emerge from a deep, dark soil—mixed and mired with social problems, economic influences, and community realities (Collins, 1971; Gamoran, 2004; Brown, 2005; Robinson & Brown, 2007). The children who arrive at the schoolhouse doors across our nation are not true *tabulae rasae* as philosophy would suggest. Children are not unscripted tablets or blank slates but complex mysteries, epic novels, and cryptic haikus. In this glib and grim context, the profession is at the crossroads of five hard questions: (1) Do we really know the difference between teaching, education, and schooling? (2) Are we cognizant of the relationship between research and teacher preparation, as well as research and teacher practice? (3) Is there congruence between what is known about how best to teach all learners and what we do to teach all students within the confines of academic policy? (4) Do we honestly account for the phenomenological and contextual differences of individual learners in our pedagogical philosophies, performances, and practices in the instruction of the many? (5) What are the short-term and long-term effects on students of teaching and/or presence in the knowledge industry?

As result of these queries, some colleges and universities have begun to structure their teacher education programs on the growing consensus related to content knowledge, pedagogical skill, and professional dispositions. NCLB requires that educators use scientifically based research to guide decisions on programs and resources to use in the classroom. This model of preparing future teachers includes reliance upon courses and majors in the arts and sciences, close coordination with practicing schools, and a focus on student cognition, particularly in reading and computation. The best science agrees that the ideal model for preparing teachers has at its core rigorous content, diagnostic assessment rubrics, developmental psychology, empirically based instructional methods, and strategies for effective classroom management.

Consequently, it should be no surprise that the empirical evidence purports a relationship between teacher/teaching characteristics and student achievement. There is unquestioned agreement in the international literature base that a teacher's experience level, subject matter knowledge, and pedagogical knowledge are correlated to student learning. The data are consistent and undisputed that there is a high correlation between a student's learning outcomes and teachers' (lack of) effectiveness and training. The question facing all professional educator preparation programs is, What kind of teachers are we producing?

Where Do We Go from Here?

The time has come for schools, colleges, and departments of education to seize this opportunity to "show and tell" the complex and critical nature of our work. We must replace teacher intuition with instructional evidence. We must systematically gather evidence to test our judgments of teaching. We must reify the importance of our jobs to civilization building, cultural development, civic engagement, the protection of democracy, and the security of our homeland. Teachers are integral players in the health and productivity of the nation (or, shall I say, good, effective teachers are integral players in the health and productivity of the nation).

In 1960, W. E. B. Du Bois spoke prophetically about post-segregated schooling in America. He warned educators that several ominous trends would result. He said "[African American] teachers will become rarer and in many cases will disappear. [African American] children will be instructed in public schools and taught under unpleasant if not discouraging circumstances. Even more largely than today they will fall out of school, cease to enter high school, and fewer and fewer will go to college" (Aptheker, 1973, p. 151). His premonition has come true. There are meaningful differences in the school experiences of the nation's students in primary, secondary, and collegiate settings. *Preparing Effective Teachers of Reading* illustrates the positive effects that can result if educators carry in their minds and hearts the intent "to leave no child behind."

The pages that follow underscore the need for equitable and comparable education for all children. Each chapter engages the policy context that governs education reform, the primacy of reading across student performance indicators, and the importance of rethinking the preparation of teachers and teacher educators. The emergent conversations center on the complex, correlated, and interwoven nexus between reading, teacher preparation, and student learning. The time has come that all teachers must know their content and be able to teach all students. Despite the national politics surrounding teaching, the power of a well-trained teacher remains the driving force of educational attainment, school reform, and student performance. In this book, we learn both what and how to teach.

References

Aptheker, H. (Ed.). (1973). *The education of black people: Ten critiques, 1906–1960*. Amherst: University of Massachusetts.

Brown, M. C. (2005). Telling the truth . . . again: Another introduction. In M. C. Brown & R. R. Land (Eds.), *The politics of curricular change: Race, hegemony and power in education* (pp. 1–11). New York: Peter Lang.

Brown, M. C., T. E. Dancy, & N. S. Norfles. (2006). A nation still at risk: No Child Left Behind and the salvation of disadvantaged students. In F. Brown & R. Hunter (Eds.), *No Child Left Behind and disadvantaged students in urban schools* (pp. 341–364). Greenwich, CT: Information Age Publishing.

Cantrell, S. C. (2002). Promoting talk: A framework for reading discussion in teacher education courses. *Journal of Adolescent & Adult Literacy*, 45, 642–651.

Cochran-Smith, M. & S. L. Lytle. (2001). Beyond certainty: Taking an inquiry stance on practice. In A. Lieberman & L. Miller (Eds.), *Teachers caught in the action: Professional development that matters*. New York: Teachers College Press, 45–58.

Collins, R. (1971). Functional and conflict theories of educational stratification. *American Sociological Review*, 36, 1000–1019.

Commeyras, M. & L. DeGroff. (1998). Literacy professionals' perspectives on professional development and pedagogy: A United States survey. *Reading Research Quarterly*, 33, 434–472.

Cuban, L. (1984). *How teachers taught: Constancy and change in American classrooms, 1890–1980*. New York: Longman.

Gamoran, A. (2004). American schooling and educational inequality: A forecast for the 21st century. In J. H. Ballantine & J. Z. Spade (Eds.), *Schools and society: A sociological approach to education* (2nd ed., pp. 249–265). Belmont, CA: Thomson Wadsworth.

Grant, R. A. & S. D. Wong. (2003). Barriers to literacy for language-minority learners: An argument for change in the literacy education profession. *Journal of Adolescent & Adult Literacy*, 46, 386–395.

Hoffman, J. & P. D. Pearson. (2000). Reading teacher education in the next millennium: What your grandmother's teacher didn't know that your granddaughter's teacher should. *Reading Research Quarterly*, 35, 28–44.

Lefever-Davis, S. (2002). The preparation of tomorrow's reading teachers. *The Reading Teacher*, 56, 196–197.

Maloch, B., J. Fine, & A. S. Flint. (2002/2003). "I just feel like I'm ready": Exploring the influence of quality teacher preparation on beginning teachers. *The Reading Teacher*, 56, 348–350.

Robinson, S. P. & M. C Brown. (Eds.). (2007). *The children Hurricane Katrina left behind: Schooling context, professional preparation, and community politics*. New York: Peter Lang.

Williams, P. J. (1991). *The alchemy of race and rights: Diary of a law professor*. Cambridge, MA: Harvard University Press.

Acknowledgments

We acknowledge the following people and organizations for their role in the conception, development, and implementation of the RFTEN project:

Deputy U.S. secretary of education 2000–2004, Bill Hansen

Dr. Michael Petrilli, associate assistant deputy secretary in the Office of Innovation and Improvement, U.S. Department of Education (position at the time of the funding)

Dr. Leonard Spearman, director of the White House Initiative on Historically Black Colleges and Universities (WHIHBCU) and former ambassador to Rwanda and Lesotho

Dr. Yvonne Maddox, deputy director, NICHD

Dr. Reid Lyon, chief of the Child Development and Behavior Branch, National Institute of Child Health and Human Development (NICHD), National Institutes of Health (NIH)

Dr. Peggy McCardle, senior advisor to the deputy director for extramural research, Office of the NIH Director

Dr. Valerie Maholmes, director of the research program in Social and Affective Development/Child Maltreatment and Violence, Child Development and Behavior Branch, NICHD

Dr. Elaine Paige Witty, dean emeritus, Norfolk State University

Dr. Beth Ann Bryant, senior advisor to the secretary of education

Dr. Lezli Baskerville, president, National Association for Equal Opportunity in Higher Education (NAFEO)

Dr. Marina Walne, consultant, U.S. Department of Education

Ms. Barbara Bolden, special assistant to the secretary of education

Dr. Carmelita Williams, past president, International Reading Association

Dr. Timothy Shanahan, president, International Reading Association

RFTEN Project Staff

Dr. Boyce C. Williams, project director, project years one, two, and three

Dr. RoSusan D. Bartee, associate director, project years two and three

Dr. Vanilla Lee, associate director, project year one

Kalisse Anderson, JD, associate director, beginning of project year two

Ms. B. Denise Hawkins, M.A., communications director, project years two and three

Mr. Alex Sorto, project manager, project year three

Ms. Barbara Jerry, administrative assistant, project years two and three

NCATE/RFTEN/NCATE Staff

Dr. Boyce C. Williams, vice president, institutional relations, NCATE

Ms. Barbara Olexer, assistant to the vice president of institutional relations, NCATE

Ms. Jane Leibbrand, vice president communications, NCATE

Ms. Jenn-Clair Kinchen, graphic artist, project years one and two

Ms. Jenna Pempek, editorial assistant/graphic design artist, project year three

RFTEN Contributors

Participating minority-serving institutions

External evaluators

Reading specialists

Quality assurance coaching consultants

National Association for Equal Opportunity in Higher Education (NAFEO)

White House Initiative on Historically Black Colleges and Universities

White House Initiative on Tribal Colleges

Hispanic Association for Colleges and Universities (HACU)

Association of Teacher Educators

National Education Association

American Federation of Teachers

American Association of Colleges for Teacher Education

The United Negro College Fund

Education Trust

Vaughn Gross Center for Reading and Language Arts

Thompson Hospitality

Educational Testing Services (ETS)

LiveText

TaskStream

National Evaluation Systems (NES)/Pearson

Norfolk State University, School of Education, Dean Jean Braxton, Norfolk, VA

North Carolina Central University, School of Education, Dean Cecelia Steppe-Jones, Durham, NC

Oglala Lakota College, School of Education, Dean Art Fisher, Kyle, SD

Frameweld, Sam Cartsos and Ashish Shah, website development and hosting

Dr. Gwendolyn Trotter, original developer of the Historically Black Colleges and Universities Technical Support Network, Vice President at Livingstone College

Dr. Alex Poinsett, consultant, Historically Black Colleges and Universities project

RFTEN

Transforming the Way Colleges Train Teachers to Teach Reading

B. DENISE HAWKINS

Language and literacy—having the tools to read, understand, learn, and comprehend—are essential to success in life and in the classroom. We know, however, that the majority of low-income and racial and ethnic minority children are not reading at a basic level by grade 4. It is imperative that we close this achievement gap. Change must begin with trained personnel teaching these students how to read. Too often, low-income and minority children attend low-performing and hard-to-staff schools where teacher turnover is a constant and where teachers have little or no training in teaching reading. Successful reading instruction begins with successful teaching programs in college.

More than half (53 percent) of African American public school teachers today earned their undergraduate degrees from Historically Black Colleges and Universities (HBCUs), and many teach predominantly Black students. However, it is hard to quantify data on teachers graduating from Hispanic-serving institutions (HSIs) and Tribal Colleges and Universities (TCUs) and where they teach.

Today, compelling research is pointing the professional teaching community toward effective teaching of reading. We know that for 90 to 95 percent of poor readers, prevention and early intervention programs work when well-trained teachers deliver scientifically based reading instructions.

Since its launch in 2003 with a $4.5 million grant from the U.S. Department of Education, the National Council for Accreditation of Teacher Education's

(NCATE) Reading First Teacher Education Network (RFTEN) has worked with a consortium of minority-serving institutions to prepare teacher candidates to be effective reading teachers. RFTEN served as the only major national initiative working with colleges of teacher education to improve reading achievement among pre-school to grade 6 (P–6) students, especially socially and economically disadvantaged children of color. At the same time, RFTEN institutions are creating adaptable models for improving reading achievement and instruction that is engaging parents, communities, and schools.

RFTEN's HBCUs, HSIs, and TCUs are demonstrating that using scientifically-based reading research (SBRR) and instruction is making a difference in the lives of candidates and students. In fact, 2,581 candidates were enrolled in SBRR courses and completed their practice teaching in 28 RFTEN institutions that have participated in all phases of the project. Those candidates provided direct instruction to more than 25,000 students, according to data gathered in 2006. These candidates were taught by 86 RFTEN/SBRR-trained faculty, who, in turn, provided instruction to more than 1,000 classroom teachers, faculty, and other educators.

The National Assessment of Educational Progress (NAEP) data show that more than 50 percent of low-income and racial and ethnic minority fourth graders are reading below a "basic" level despite national efforts to bridge the widening achievement gap in reading. The situation is dire, and reading scores among these children show little sign of improving. The RFTEN project took the road less traveled, focusing on creating successful and informed teaching programs in colleges and believing that these were the places where effective reading instruction must begin.

Since 2003, RFTEN, in collaboration with NCATE, the National Institute for Child Health and Human Development, and the Vaughn Gross Center for Reading and Language Arts at the University of Texas, Austin (2003–2005), has partnered with college presidents, deans, and faculty to improve the technical and instructional skills of those charged with teaching reading in elementary schools. RFTEN incorporated research findings—identified by the National Research Panel and underlying federal "Reading First" grants—into the base of faculty knowledge, courses, supplementary materials, and clinical and practical teaching experiences of candidates for elementary teaching. In 2006, NCATE concluded its administration of the RFTEN grant.

The design and delivery of the RFTEN project set into motion a fresh approach to responding to the reading crisis among young children. This is just the beginning.

RFTEN: Investing in Young Lives

It is critical that teachers graduating from minority-serving institutions have the knowledge and skills to reach disadvantaged, low-income, and racial and ethnic minority children. Intervention that includes changes in reading curricula at the pre-service level is the most efficient way to train these future teachers. The 2005 NAEP data continue to show gaps in the area of reading. Despite improvement in Black and Hispanic student performance for grades 4 and 8, scores for White students were about 30 points higher. The achievement gap in reading did not change significantly from 1992 to 2005 for grades 4 and 8.

RFTEN helped to ensure that candidates know and understand how to use evidence-based strategies to teach reading to elementary students so that all children can read at grade level by grade 3. Many of the thirty-eight selected RFTEN institutions did not have reading specialist programs, as these are advanced-level programs of study, and the institutions in question were baccalaureate institutions. But graduates from these institutions will likely be the ones teaching minority and disadvantaged children enrolled in Reading First, hard-to-staff, and low-performing schools.

The RFTEN project represents an investment in the lives of minority children and their communities. It is one of the Department of Education's approaches to implementing reading instruction and is supported by a strong body of research. RFTEN has been able to tap into the successes of NCATE's earlier partnerships including the HBCU Network, a foundation-supported project that assisted selected institutions with preparations for NCATE accreditation.

Behind RFTEN is the belief that to change policies, minds must first be changed. The project employed a two-part process: first, with the help of NCATE, RFTEN worked to gain support for change within faculty and university leadership by engaging presidents and deans in supporting the project to teach reading using new resources and approaches. Second, it engaged faculty in realigning reading instruction with evidence-based research and provided them with a series of professional development opportunities and collaborative seminars and instructional materials, as well as access to reading experts and technical consultants. Those resources are helping equip faculty as they align their course curricula and other teacher preparation programs with effective evidence-based practices in reading.

How RFTEN Impacts Institutions

RFTEN has also helped foster and enhance community and higher education collaboration.

"To me, support and commitment to the RFTEN project has meant that Alcorn State University could not have an effective teacher education program without first having strong reading instruction as its foundation," said Dr. Clinton Bristow Jr., the late president of Alcorn State University in Lorman, Mississippi. Commitment from college presidents has been critical to the success of the project. When he chaired RFTEN's first presidential advisory board, Dr. Norman Francis, president of Xavier University in New Orleans, said that presidents and senior-level academic administrators "must be engaged in improving reading instruction in our institutions."

Through such partnerships, faculty and teaching candidates use scientifically based tool sets and implement what they learned from online teaching and networking experiences with their colleagues in the project. As the RFTEN project is supported by NCATE, it is important to consider how the project might impact NCATE accreditation in general. Dr. Arthur E. Wise, president of NCATE, states that in the early years NCATE specified inputs into the education process. NCATE then began to focus on the curriculum and to inspect colleges to see whether their written curricula matched the agency's standards. In 2001, NCATE began judging the degree to which colleges could provide data showing that candidates have the required knowledge, skills, and ability to be effective teachers.

In fact, many of the project's partner institutions have used RFTEN resources. Their participation in this national initiative has been a springboard for changing how they, the community, parents, and local schools support reading achievement and prepare trained reading teachers.

2006: RFTEN's Final Year—
Implications for NCATE and Reading Instruction

The 2006 academic year marked the culmination of RFTEN's efforts to intervene at the preservice level to ensure that teacher candidates know and understand how to use evidence-based reading strategies to teach and support reading achievement, especially among children enrolled in low-performing, hard-to-staff, and Reading First schools. That year also marked RFTEN's evaluation, an important and multipronged process that documented the project and demonstrated its impact on teaching, learning, and communities. The evaluation explores and documents standards for what is taught and what is tested in the curriculum to make sure they are congruent.

One key evaluation finding is that "[i]t is quite possible—maybe even probable—that candidates can be licensed to teach elementary students in 2006 without demonstrating their knowledge of essential components of reading instruction derived from research," according to the RFTEN report "Licensure Alignment with the Essential Components of Effective Reading Instruction." The report, prepared by Dr. Diana W. Rigden, who was then a senior associate at the American Association of Colleges for Teacher Education, is pivotal to the RFTEN evaluation. The report examines the alignment of state licensure tests with the statutory definition of "essential components of reading instruction" (defined in the No Child Left Behind Act of 2001 as phonemic awareness, phonics, vocabulary development, reading fluency, including oral reading skills, and reading comprehension strategies); and the correspondence of NCATE/Specialty Professional Association standards with these essential reading components.

The RFTEN project has reaffirmed the importance of national accreditation in maintaining accountability in teacher education programs, learning, and reading achievement. In addition, RFTEN has provided a lens through which NCATE has been able to explore how well, and in what ways, its expectations for teacher knowledge and skills and assessment evidence gathered on candidates' proficiencies are aligned with the SBRR principles underlying RFTEN.

The rubrics used in NCATE Unit Standard One require programs to think about what candidates know and are able to do at the individual course level. Reading-content faculty must also be able to identify where in the early childhood/elementary education reading curriculum SBRR is covered and how it will be applied. Faculty members are expected to model best practice and collaborate with P–6 schools. This way, RFTEN faculty are able to assess a candidate's skill set in the use of SBRR and provide opportunities for children to have multiple professionals working with them using a common knowledge base.

The active participation of presidents, deans, and faculty at RFTEN partner institutions has propelled this project in unparalleled ways. In year three came the realization that the RFTEN project, through NCATE, has numerous implications for the profession and for the way data and evidence are collected and analyzed to show impact on student learning and on closing the achievement gap in reading.

A Sampling of Campus Results from RFTEN

California State University–Northridge

Students at elementary schools who are taught by teacher candidates from this RFTEN institution have passed the California State Reading Assessment at all grade levels. Findings reveal that 90 percent of all teacher candidates trained in SBRR have been successful on the state's Reading Licensure Exam.

Florida International University (Miami, Florida)

Successful Florida International University graduates trained in the RFTEN/SBRR model are part of a pilot research project to determine how effective first-year teachers are in the classroom and whether they are having an effect on student reading achievement. All teacher candidates have been reported as being successful on Praxis exams—teacher certification exams written and administered by the Educational Testing Service.

Oglala Lakota College (Kyle, South Dakota)

Using a RFTEN-sponsored Summer Reading Institute in 2005, Oglala Lakota College, located on the Pine Ridge Reservation in South Dakota, brought together more than 60 teachers, teacher candidates, and principals representing Bureau of Indian Affairs schools. This first-ever professional forum on reading also engaged parents and families. A second successful Reading Institute was held in 2006.

Alcorn State University (Alcorn State, Mississippi)

Children in a low-performing partner school taught by preservice teachers trained in the RFTEN/SBBR model increased their scores on a state achievement exam from Level 3 to Level 5.

Alabama State University (Montgomery, Alabama)

Candidates trained in SBRR from this institution in Montgomery, Alabama, are reporting gains among the children they are teaching in their partner Reading First schools.

Campus Feedback (based on RFTEN Evaluation findings)

From Reading Faculty

"RFTEN Collaborative Development Seminars (CDSs) provided opportunities to gather new information related to SBRR and collaborate with other reading faculty."

From Presidents

"Advance the premise that the teaching of reading should be guided by a structured curriculum."

"Increased skills and knowledge-based concepts among faculty and thereby encourage the use of the most current methodology in teacher education programs."

"Provide enhanced professional development for the respective faculty."

RFTEN is also:

- reclaiming the legacy of HBCUs and the promises for teaching at HSIs and TCUs in the production of African American, Hispanic, and Indian teachers.
- redirecting conversations about student learning outcomes related to teacher quality and teacher education programs, a shared responsibility between the public and higher education.
- reemphasizing the importance of top-down leadership in supporting higher education outcomes.
- redefining "how teachers teach" and "how students learn" in the spirit of No Child Left Behind.
- reaffirming the importance of national accreditation in maintaining accountability in teacher education programs.

CHAPTER ONE

The HBCU Technical Support Network

A Bridge to RFTEN

BOYCE C. WILLIAMS

One of the gravest challenges facing historically black colleges and universities (HBCUs), Hispanic-serving institutions (HSIs), and tribal colleges and universities (TCUs) today is how to preserve their long tradition of educating black, Hispanic, and Native American teachers in the face of new educational reforms.

As HBCUs, HSIs, and TCUs have evolved in recent decades, they have wrestled with the need to link their tradition of building collaborative alliances with the implementation of systematic planning for the future. Effective education of teachers and educational leaders has become one of the cherished traditions, and an important part of the mission, of minority-serving institutions. The Historically Black Colleges and Universities Technical Support Network (HBCUTSN) was created to assist HBCUs in carrying out their mission. With support from the Lilly Endowment, Inc., and the Mott Foundation in 1995, the HBCUTSN set out to strengthen teacher preparation programs at HBCUs. To do that, the HBCUTSN developed a four-part technical assistance model that incorporated assessment, education, coaching, and collaboration. The model served as the foundation for RFTEN, a three-year grant initiative sponsored by the U.S. Department of Education to transform teacher preparation in reading at selected minority-serving institutions. Like the HBCU Network, the RFTEN project operated on strong principles of collaboration. This chapter describes the basic elements of the collaboration phase in the HBCUTSN model.

HBCUs and a Plan for Collaboration

The HBCU collaboration, the fourth component of the HBCUTSN model, was designed to move an institution toward systemic change. This section discusses the major strategies employed during the model's collaborative phase.

"Collaboration" has become a buzzword in recent discussions on educational reform. To realize benefits, however, we must remove the obstacles that have prevented collaborative efforts from succeeding. One of those obstacles is the practice of working independently, rather than interdependently, even when the goals of different organizations or different units within a single organization are similar. Roland Barth likens our noncollaborative tendencies to the "parallel play" of children:

> Two three-year olds are busily engaged in opposite corners of a sandbox. One has a shovel and bucket; one has a rake and hoe. At no time do they share each other's tools. Although in proximity and having much to offer one another, each works and plans pretty much in isolation. (1996, p. 6)

To a great extent, the age-old problem of gaps between knowledge and theory, or research and practice, can be attributed to failures to collaborate in matters that are obviously related. Barth calls for dual citizenship for teachers and teacher educators in schools and colleges, arguing that collaboration in teaching of preservice professionals will serve to bridge gaps between what students are taught and the application of that knowledge in the classroom.

A second obstacle is the absence of collegiality. Jay Robinson sees the lack of collegiality as reflecting misplaced priorities. He argues that a new kind of collegiality is needed to overcome institutionalized separations born of difference in status. His discussion makes clear the importance of the human side of things, not only for colleagues in colleges and schools but also in our work with students.

In a very practical sense, the traditional reward system of higher education is another obstacle. Colleges inadvertently discourage partnerships with and services to P–12 schools by assigning low status to those who work with these schools. This environment makes it difficult to sustain collaborative relationships.

Redefining Collaboration

It was important to differentiate between the past experiences of HBCUs with collaborative ventures and the types of ventures that the collaborative component of the HBCUTSN model envisioned. Redefining collaboration was an important first step:

Collaboration is a much used and abused word. Unexamined, it suggests that whatever tasks are to be done can be done equally well by all participants. . . . We mean neither an unthinking acceptance of the view that all partners in an activity are equally fit to do all things, nor a elitist view that one group has wisdom and experience superior to the other. We posit an idea yet to be realized: collaboration that capitalizes on the research and experience of the best professors in the academy and on the expertise and experience of the best teachers in the schools, recognizing that valuable attributes reside in both places. (*HBCUTSN Handbook*, p. 64)

This definition distinguishes past experiences and cooperative initiatives from current ones by calling attention to the need for a proactive stance in planning collaborations for excellence. The essential goal of collaboration in the HBCUTSN model was to facilitate interdependent work among HBCUs and to encourage self-sufficiency.

Through collaboration, institutions share resources with on campus colleagues and with other institutions that are preparing for accreditation reviews. Collaboration enhances the capacity of institutions to: (1) identify resources they may need from other sources in the education community, (2) establish a professional development network to promote self-generated improvement of teacher education programs, and (3) serve as resources for other institutions undergoing accreditation reviews or program changes.

1. Collaboration must be planned.
2. Collaborative activities must have a shared vision.
3. Collaborative activities must have a shared language.
4. Collaboration is built on trust and understanding.

Beginning with Assessment

The needs assessment component of the HBCU Network had two levels; the first is identification of the literal or functional needs through direct investigation and review of evidence. This process is underpinned by a larger general need for building the fundamental capability of the unit to remedy identified weaknesses. Analysis of the National Council for Accreditation of Teacher Education (NCATE) accreditation standards shows that they were often not met by HBCUs because of issues around (in order of frequency and in terms of the NCATE standards): (1) resources, (2) faculty qualifications, (3) faculty development, (4) relationships with schools, and (5) faculty load.

HBCU Network consultants found that institutions needed to strengthen three major dimensions: the development of resources, the development of professional networks, and the development of professional foundations.

Developing Resources:
Extending the Assessment Component

Resource development is linked to the assessment phase of the HBCU Network facilitation model, which helps identify which program elements and program documentation should be revised or strengthened. It also helps create consensus among faculty within and outside of the professional education unit on the rationale for and direction of needed changes.

We can examine some of the problems attributed to limited resources and consider ways that strategic planning for collaboration could aid HBCUs: (1) problems surrounding recruitment, admission, retention, and career placement of teacher candidates; (2) employability problems associated with testing for admission and certification; and (3) documentation problems undergirded by inadequacies in systems for storing, retrieving, and using data for reporting and assessing the progress of students and programs. It is clear that a strategic plan should include collaboration that allows the teacher education unit to capitalize on the existing resources of other units whose functions overlap with its own (e.g., recruitment, admissions, assessment, counseling, and career placement services).

External resources are too often considered the concern of the campus development office. The teacher education unit should work closely with the development office in searching for external funds. The teacher education unit should be able to communicate its needs and assist the development office in writing proposals that address the goals and needs of the unit. In the past, funding opportunities for teacher education programs have not been attractive to development officials, as the amount of money allocated in the area of teacher education has often been low in comparison with the amount allocated to other academic areas. Where funds are larger, for example in math and science education, professionals in the content discipline rather than teacher educators who focus on the pedagogy of the content are often selected to play the lead role in projects. In addition, when funds are secured without appropriate communication with the teacher education unit, the nature of the funded projects may not be in keeping with the goals of the unit, resulting in add-ons that increase the workload of an already understaffed area. Larger institutions often resolve these problems by establishing full-time positions for development professionals. This is difficult for smaller institutions like HBCUs.

A strategic plan for collaboration must consider ways to strengthen communication about the teacher education program and to foster collaboration between teacher education units and development offices for joint resource development activities. Minimally, such a plan should include mechanisms for ensuring that the acquisition of external funds supports the goals and conceptual framework of the teacher education unit.

Developing Professional Networks: Extending the Educative Component

In the educative phase of the model, special attention was given to professional development activities, which were driven largely by the needs assessment. Beyond the basics of reviewing the curriculum and initiating faculty development activities for the teacher education unit, the collaboration component focused on building professional communities to support the ongoing process of learning. Emphasis was placed on establishing systems for continuous improvement in curriculum restructuring, professional development, and linkages between knowledge and practice. The underlying assumptions are that (1) the teacher education knowledge base is and will always be in a state of growth and (2) educators will be continuously involved in advancing the knowledge base for teaching.

Concerns about the quality of instruction in schools are directly related to the quality of teachers. As noted by Goodlad (1990), for reform efforts to be successful, we must have "simultaneous renewal" of schools and teacher preparation programs. The move toward simultaneous renewal is undergirded by a recognition of the two-dimensional nature of curriculum restructuring and professional development. The professional network element of collaboration uses the axiom "Practice what you teach and teach what you practice." In other words, restructuring the curriculum carries with it the obligation for teacher educators to use the effective practices they talk about. It has often been said that students are more likely to teach as they were taught than to teach as they were taught to teach. If we restructure teacher education programs, we must also provide opportunities for professional development so that faculty can deliver effective instruction. Of particular interest, then, are (1) joint professional development and curriculum development programs within the institution involving the teacher education unit and academic units in the arts and sciences and (2) the development of professional networks for teacher educators and teachers.

With joint professional development and curriculum restructuring, the work on learning communities provides models for adaptation most compatible with the major design features of the collaboration model presented here. Evolving models of learning communities embrace basic concepts associated with contemporary pedagogical reform efforts. Further learning communities may be created for both curriculum development and professional development. By their very nature, learning communities embrace the notions of cooperation, coordination, and communication (Gablenick, MacGregor, Matthews, & Smith, 1990). In other words, learning communities can be a vehicle for addressing faculty issues such as lack of intellectual vitality, intellectual isolation, and inflexible reward systems.

In terms of professional networks between teacher educators and teachers, the evolving work on professional development schools provides models to inform the development of strategic plans, particularly with regard to bridging the gap between the knowledge acquired in teacher education programs and of the application of that knowledge in the classroom. The professional development school movement has many sources, but of special interest to this model is the laboratory school that was so common in early HBCUs. The teacher educator taught in both the college and the school, giving her the responsibility of naturally bridging the knowledge/application gap and modeling effective teaching strategies for the person in training. Because today's structures lend themselves better to partnerships between two people, one from college and one from school, we are more likely to approach the dual responsibilities for preprofessionals' knowledge and performance through partnerships between teachers and teacher educators. As work evolved on professional development schools, effective practices were developed, including (1) an emphasis on longer and more substantive clinical experiences, (2) teaching exchanges for college- and school-based educators, and (3) joint research between teachers and teacher educators.

Developing Professional Foundations: Extending Coaching

In the coaching phase of the HBCUTSN model, attention was given to documenting and reviewing an institution's activities. Collaboration extends coaching to include information sharing. Potential areas for partnership include the sharing of information within the institution, among HBCUs, and between teacher education units and preschool–grade 12 (P–12) schools. These are examples of the collaborative efforts that have evolved through the implementation of various phases of the HBCUTSN model. The intention is to make information available to others, especially HBCUs, about effective strategies for enhancing teacher education programs. The second aim is to use electronic databases for sharing information. In addition, traditional services that might be considered include public forums, publications, and demonstration centers, all with a focus on effective collaboration strategies.

Beyond these models will be other opportunities to provide services in response to specific needs. For example, there has been a call for colleges to provide services to school districts to help them implement changes called for in legislation or in their own school or district plans. Higher education institutions cannot make unilateral decisions about the needs of P–12 schools: for productive engagement, all participants must enter the relationship having clearly identified what they need and what they are giving to and receiving from the collaboration.

Using a strategic plan for collaboration, the unit can enhance its capacity (1) to identify and develop resources it may need from other sources in the education community, (2) to establish professional networks to promote improvement of teacher education programs, and (3) to serve as a resource for other higher education institutions and schools involved in improving the quality of education. In other words, during the collaborative phase of the technical assistance model, the institution is becoming adept at building an infrastructure for systemic change in three areas: resource development, clinical programs, and professional networking.

In building an infrastructure, it is clearly not enough to point to fragments of the collaborative puzzle, addressing needs one by one. We need to look toward the "big picture"—not only where we want to go but how we can get there. Furthermore, schools and universities should be able to document and report the types of collaboration that work well in addressing educational improvements. It follows that the major goal of the collaborative component is to assist HBCUs in developing strategic plans for collaboration in the areas of resource development, professional networking, and service development.

Guiding Principles for Developing Strategic Plans for Collaboration

Five basic principles will guide the development of strategic plans for collaboration. It is important to make the strategic plans of the institution and the teacher education unit the focal point for the strategic plans for collaboration. Typically, strategic plans describe long-term goals, usually five years, and short-term goals, which are annual targets or indicators for achieving incremental changes. We are confronted with the challenge of aligning the institutional strategic plan with the plans of its individual units. For example, the strategic plans for teacher education units must both complement the institutional plan and reflect the requirements of accrediting agencies.

Some educational reform specialists have concluded that change from the top down and the bottom up must take place simultaneously (Fullan, 1993). A common viewpoint about the failure of a change effort is that collaboration members do not have knowledge of or practice with systematic problem solving, shared planning, or shared responsibilities—elements that go into effective collaboration. Therefore, the second principle is that participants must be trained in effective strategies for collaboration.

If strategic plans for collaboration are to be successful, consideration must be given to the needs of the teacher education unit and their relationship to the strategic goals of the teacher education unit and to the institution. The institution must know clearly how it, as a whole, will benefit from collaborative efforts of teacher education and other units. Furthermore, we must acknowledge that benefits derived will involve other units on campus. Therefore, the third principle is that key partners must be involved in developing and implementing the strategic plan.

Discussions of collaboration tend to focus on partnerships between universities or schools and external constituents. Far less attention is given to partnerships within the institution, resulting in the failure to see many opportunities for maximizing existing resources. The fourth principle is that strategic plans for collaboration must consider collaboratives both within the institution and between the institution and external groups.

In the interest of systemic change, the fifth principle is that strategic plans for collaboration will actively seek ways of integrating related functions across units. This means accepting from the outset that reengineering or restructuring may be the most reasonable way to address some problems. Such redesign may take formal avenues (restructured departments), transitional approaches (reassignment of faculty time within existing structures), or informal routes (cross-collaboration among faculty and students).

It cannot be overemphasized that the intention of the collaborative component of the HBCUTSN model was to provide the type of technical support that would enhance the overall effectiveness of teacher education units. HBCUs were assisted in the development of strategic plans for collaboration to meet the challenge of preserving their long tradition of educating teachers. The launch in 2003 of the RFTEN project, administered by NCATE, extended the reach of the successful HBCUTSN model. As a result, the RFTEN grant, which concluded in September 2006, targeted a specific content area (reading) and implemented the HBCU Network model as it transformed the way teacher educators at TCUs, HSIs, and HBCUs prepared teachers to teach reading. In fact, professional development for these education faculties, teaching exchanges for college and school-based educators, college/school partnerships, the collaboration of university and school professionals, and the creation of an online professional network for the exchange of information and resources were among the concepts and practices gleaned from the HBCU Network model and became hallmarks of the RFTEN project.

References

Barth, R. (1996). "School and University: Bad Dreams, Good Dreams." *On Common Ground: Yale-New Haven Teachers Institute,* 6 (Spring). (pp. 1, 5–7).

Committee on Policy for Racial Justice. (1989). *Visions of a better way: A black appraisal of public schooling.* Washington, DC: Joint Center for Political Studies Press.

Consultant Guide for Assessment. (1996). Historically Black Colleges and Universities Teacher Education Technical Support Network. Washington, DC: NCATE.

Fullan, M. (1993). "Innovation, Reform, and Restructuring Strategies." In *Challenges and Achievement in American Education.* G. Cawelti (Ed.), 1993 Yearbook of the Association for Supervision and Curriculum Development (pp. 116–133). Alexandria, VA: ASCD.

Gablenick, F., Jean MacGregor, Roberta Matthews, and Barbara Lee Smith. (1990). *Learning Communities: Creating Connections among Students, Faculty, and Disciplines.* New Directions for Teaching and Learning, no. 41. San Francisco: Jossey-Bass.

Goodlad, J.I. (1990). *Teachers for our nation's schools.* San Francisco: Jossey-Bass.

Robinson, J. (1996). "University-School Collaboration and Education Reform." *On Common Ground. Yale-New Haven Teachers Institute,* 6 (Spring). (pp. 14–15).

Resources

It is important to note while not directly quoted, the following references serve as the historical backdrop for developing the network:

Clark, S. (1990). *Ready from within,* African World. Lawrenceville, NJ.

Clewell, B. C. & B. T. Anderson. (1995). "African Americans in Higher Education: An Issue of Access." *Humboldt Journal of Social Relations,* Vol. 21 (2) (pp. 55–79).

Dilworth, M. (1984). *Teachers' totter: A report of teacher certification issues.* Washington, DC: Howard University, Institute for the Study of Educational Policy.

Though not directly quoted, the foundation for the RFTEN model can be found in the Price Pritchett series including *The Employee Handbook for Organizational Change* (2006) and *Firing Up Commitment During Organizational Change: A Handbook for Managers* (1994), Dallas, Texas.

CHAPTER TWO

RFTEN and the Role of Collaboration

RFTEN and the Role of the Reading Consultant

BRIAN R. BRYANT

National reading consultants were an integral part of the RFTEN project model. They functioned largely as collaborative colleagues to the faculty at their assigned RFTEN partner institutions, and their specific duties were outlined in the *RFTEN Consultant Handbook* as follows:

- Conduct consultative, planning, and information-gathering site visits to various participating colleges.
- Deliver technical assistance to participating higher education faculty.
- Deliver professional development on topics related to scientifically based reading research (SBRR).
- Provide expert advice on implementing SBRR materials into course content and application into syllabi for preservice teachers.
- Conduct observations.
- Document activities that establish contact with participating faculty (e.g., phone calls, letters, and emails).
- Document substantive conversations via email and phone (e.g., phone calls to help plan reading workshops).

As fellow professionals, RFTEN participants and their consultants shared one primary characteristic. They were all faculty members responsible for guiding students through an exhaustive academic process. Usually lasting 4 or 5 years, this educational process is designed to transform teacher candidates from individuals "who want to make a difference in children's lives" into professionals who will have the tools to make a difference in children's lives when they teach children to read using SBRR.

Before embarking on their scheduled visits with RFTEN faculty members, reading consultants were encouraged to learn about their assigned campuses to understand better the climate, culture, history, students, and surrounding community.

For example, one consultant visited Bethune-Cookman College in Daytona Beach, Florida. Before doing so, he took time to go to the college's Web site to learn about the campus and its history. What he found was most intriguing:

> The year was 1904 when a very determined young Black woman, Mary McLeod Bethune, opened the Daytona Educational and Industrial Training School for Negro Girls. It underwent several stages of growth and development through the years. In 1923, it became a coed high school as a result of a merger with Cookman Institute of Jacksonville, Florida. A year later, the school became affiliated with the United Methodist Church, evolved into a junior college by 1931 and became known as Bethune-Cookman College.

According to another source (http://www.africawithin.com/bios/mary_bethune.htm), the initial school population consisted of five girls and Mrs. Bethune's son. From such humble beginnings, Bethune-Cookman College was formed, and the consultant found that Mrs. Bethune's vision for young people, as reinforced in the school's mission statement, has remained in place to this day.

> The mission is to serve in the Christian tradition the educational, social, and cultural needs of its students—traditional and nontraditional—and to develop in them the desire and capacity for continuous intellectual and professional growth, leadership, and service to others. Institutional priorities in the mission of the College are teaching, research, community service and commitment to moral and personal values.

During the visit to see the instructor, the consultant met with students, many of whom were first-generation college students—the first member of their extended family to attend college. The consultant shared the value of educators and asked students whether there was one teacher they had as youngsters who helped change their lives. All of the students raised their hands, and several shared their stories. Later, one student was asked to take the consultant to Mrs. Bethune's resting place on campus. As they walked, the student shared how he had been kicked out of high school in inner-city New York. One teacher visited his home and spent time talking with the student about his future. The student had a decision to make. Would he drop out of school or dedicate himself to securing his future by returning to school and doing what was necessary to graduate? The student told the consultant that he went back to school, stayed out of trouble, and graduated. And now he would soon be graduating from Bethune-Cookman. He also shared that he would be returning home soon on break and had decided to stop by the school and thank his former teacher for making a difference in his life.

Mrs. Bethune saw the potential in young people and worked to give them the opportunity to thrive. This is the legacy of this education pioneer and is the spirit that pervades the campus. In the Historically Black College and University community, there are other institutions like Bethune-Cookman. Similarly, many RFTEN partner institutions have similar stories and a campus culture that is integral to understanding its faculty, its students, and its alumni. And because a campus exists within a community of learners, surrounded by neighborhood schools where teacher candidates will have their field experiences, the culture of the community plays a critical role in the successful training of these future educators. By gaining an understanding, however cursory, of these intermingling cultures, reading consultants can better meet the needs of their colleagues at RFTEN institutions.

How do reading consultants meet the needs of their RFTEN colleagues? First, consultants are informed and guided by needs assessments completed by RFTEN participants. These assessments were conducted when RFTEN instructors met for scheduled professional development events. On the basis of survey results, consultants were able to examine several key areas of need, including materials, assessment, classroom observation, collegial assistance, Higher Education Collaborative (HEC) Online, SBRR integration, field placements, and syllabi. The remainder of this chapter looks at each area by describing its relevance to the RFTEN project, providing topical anecdotal comments made by consultants during their site visits, and, when relevant, citing data collected to examine the topic's importance with regard to the project.

Materials

RFTEN members were given an abundance of instructional and resource materials before and during professional development events known as collaborative development seminars. It was apparent from the needs assessments, however, that RFTEN faculty members would need assistance in identifying how to incorporate the materials they received into their classes. The needs assessment survey item read as follows: "Faculty in preservice programs should have materials related to scientifically based reading instruction to use in their reading/language arts courses." Over 85 percent of the instructors agreed with this statement.

The Vaughn Gross Center for Reading and Language Arts (VGCRLA) at the University of Texas, Austin, had been creating SBRR-related professional development materials for years and made these materials available to RFTEN members. Using the slides/overheads and handouts, RFTEN faculty could explain what the five areas of reading were, present guidelines for how to teach each area effectively, demonstrate actual reading lessons, and, in the case of the struggling readers materials, show their students how to make instructional adaptations.

Consultants often provided technical assistance to faculty members and sometimes modeled lectures to students. Here are a few comments made by consultants regarding materials, from their consultant reports:

> I visited the classroom, a computer lab, and noted where materials are kept for students to have immediate access; there is a checkout system in place. Since this is a computer lab, the instructors utilize the RFTEN CDs for class presentations.

> I noted that several RFTEN materials have been placed online for students to access. The students download the information and place them in the Literacy Resource Notebook.

> I spent some time talking about some of the materials that are available through the Reading Center, including information on struggling readers and family literacy. Because one instructor deals with reading in special education, we also spent some time discussing the Secondary Special Education Reading Project's (SERP's) institutes for students who are blind or hearing impaired or deaf and hard of hearing. I mentioned that I would share some of the materials with them, but I also mentioned that many of the resources are available online.

> I was given a tour of the Education building, most notably their in-building library resource center for students. In this spacious room, students have access to basal reading series, children's books, and multimedia resources. I mentioned the importance of providing various types of text (e.g., patterned, predictable, decodable, authentic) so that students can see the differences among text types and be able to match texts to each learner.

> The Livingstone Reading First room is a wonderful example of how RFTEN resources were used effectively. In the room, which also serves as a classroom, are a variety of reading texts (e.g., patterned texts, early readers), posters, textbooks, and materials that have been purchased with RFTEN monies. Students can see how SBRR is translated into practice and can have hands-on experiences with materials that have been proven to be effective. The room is filled with reminders that all children need to be able to read and that reading is not restricted to books but also includes maps, newspapers, and other print material. It was very impressive, and we talked at some length as to how the participant was using the room with her classes. It was quite impressive.

Another instructor teaches reading in the content areas. She was most interested in the SERP materials and the IDEA 04 and Research for Inclusive Settings (IRIS) website. All three faculty indicated that the Online Teacher Reading Academies (OTRAs), which I demonstrated as they had not been reviewed before this meeting, would be very helpful in their instruction. I demonstrated how to view the videos, download handouts, review references, etc.

During the next academic year, the faculty will include the OTRAs as part of their syllabi. They feel that the various activities and handouts included in the OTRAs will provide their candidates great insight regarding strategies that support reading. They also plan to develop a "teaching center," designed by the candidates and faculty, which will include the use of OTRAs in the technology area.

I attended the RFTEN Resource Room Dedication refreshments on Wednesday at 5:30. A number of students showed up as did faculty whom I did not recognize. I said a few words about how this could serve as a model for sharing resources. I think it was a great way to spend their money—really provides a place and opportunity to share the materials that they have been given with their students and their faculty. They even got some matching funds from somewhere in the college to purchase a SmartBoard. I look forward—on my return visit—to seeing how the RR is being used and what system they have devised for checking out materials.

During their work with RFTEN, faculty members rated the extent to which the materials (1) enhanced their own knowledge of reading and how to teach reading and (2) provided valuable information for the instructors to use in their courses. The data indicate that the materials achieved both objectives. This is particularly important because most faculty members are uncomfortable teaching content that they are unfamiliar with or have little knowledge of. Increasing the RFTEN faculty members' knowledge, therefore, makes it more likely that they will find the material of value to their students and include the materials in their courses. We saw this demonstrated in the survey results.

Assessments

Practicing teachers need to be able to administer reading assessments and use the results to inform their instruction. Questions such as "What should I teach?," "Are the students learning?," and "What evidence do I have that students are making adequate yearly progress as demanded by No Child Left Behind legislation?" can all be answered only by collecting and interpreting assessment data.

The needs assessment asked RFTEN members to respond to the statement that "preservice teachers should know how to use assessment data to inform instruction." More than 90 percent of the members agreed that knowledge about reading assessment is an important skill for teachers to possess, and consultants provided technical assistance about a variety of assessment topics. One consultant described an opportunity she had to provide technical assistance:

> <Participant> shared with me samples of the individual progress reports that practicum students are required to create for submission to the professors and to the parents of the students with whom they work. For each struggling reader, practicum students create a portfolio that they submit electronically that includes basic student information, affective information (i.e., reading attitude or interest surveys, student responses, and a written summary of student's attitude and interests), a parent interview, an informal reading interview (i.e., graded word lists with student responses and/or graded passages with miscues marked, comprehension questions and retelling score sheet with student responses, a summary of student's oral reading performance, a miscue tally and reading behavior summary charts, and a summary of student's comprehension performance on the basic reading inventory), a formal assessment (i.e., DIBELS [Dynamic Indicators of Basic Early Literacy Skills]), informal assessments consisting of pre- and posttest writing samples and spelling assessments, parent and student meetings with documentation, a final summary (addressing student growth, addressing the initial and ending assessment), a prescriptive plan based on assessment and identifying student strengths and needs with goals and objectives matching assessments, daily lesson plans based on the prescriptive plan, a parent report that gives a summary of student progress, an outline of the prescriptive plan and includes recommendations for parents, a student portfolio including work samples, journals, and assignments, and a final summary focusing on student growth and addressing the pre- and post-testing.

Many instructors purchased tests with money allocated for materials. One instructor brought out a test and asked her consultant for technical assistance on its administration and scoring. Because the consultant happened to be one of the authors of the test she inquired about, technical assistance was easily given.

Course Syllabi

In higher education, the course syllabus provides a road map for faculty members and students. Each course syllabus provides goals and objectives for the course, information about the text that will be used as primary and secondary information resources, topics of each meeting date, student responsibilities, and so forth. Thus, reading course syllabi provide a snapshot of the philosophical and pedagogical underpinnings of what is being taught and how.

> After all of the students left, I looked at the instructor's syllabi. The instructor had already revised her syllabi after attending the RFTEN meetings in Washington, DC. I made a few suggestions for including more fluency content within her syllabus. Mrs. Cuff, another instructor at the campus, had not been involved with the RFTEN so there

were many suggestions I shared with her. Both instructors were very receptive and open to incorporating my suggestions. When I returned in April they would show me a revised copy of their syllabi.

Ethel had scheduled a syllabi work session for faculty and Cynthia had brought two of her syllabi (one undergraduate, one graduate). However, the needs of the group seemed to be other than working on syllabi . . . we discussed the latest research in the areas of ELL and struggling readers and I shared a number of resources with the faculty.

Her syllabus indicated that she incorporates the five components throughout the course work.

I reviewed their course syllabi and gave them suggestions for implementation of SBRR in the syllabi.

Melba has created a syllabus that is aligned with all of the components of SBRR and follows the guidelines given to her by RFTEN.

All members were asked to submit their course syllabi to the RFTEN staff for examination. The extent to which the syllabi included SBRR and desired RFTEN features was conveyed to each faculty member. Helpful feedback was given to support faculty members as they worked to align their syllabi with RFTEN objectives. Consultants received copies of the feedback to members, and the majority received good marks on the basis of their inclusion of the five core areas of reading and of SBRR.

When RFTEN participants were asked to improve and resubmit their syllabi after constructive feedback from reading consultants, there was a marked improvement, even for faculty members whose initial syllabi received high marks. Analyses by the program evaluation staff determined that the improvement was statistically significant, demonstrating the instructors' commitment to the project and its goals.

Classroom Observations

Classroom observations provide a view of what is actually being taught and how. Does the faculty member provide lectures only, or are students allowed to interact with faculty and with one another? How is each of the five main areas of reading taught? What roles do handouts, materials, and visuals play in the college/university classroom? These and many similar questions can be answered only by sitting in a classroom and watching faculty members teach reading content to their students.

Meeting with RFTEN faculty members afforded the reading consultants the unique opportunity to gather information on the extent to which SBRR was being integrated into college coursework. On many occasions, consultants were able to sit in on classes and see the integration for themselves.

One RFTEN faculty member is at North Carolina Central University in Durham, North Carolina. As part of my consultant responsibilities, I observed her teaching one of her reading courses.

Tonight's lecture focused on phonological awareness, one of the five key instructional components supported by RFTEN and SBRR. There were seventeen students in the class, and all seemed to be attentive and involved in the class.

The session began with a cartoon of Dr. Martin Luther King Jr. asking a parent leaving a mall with a child (who had all kinds of the current "gear" that was purchased during the shopping trip), "Did you buy him a book?" This provided an excellent advance organizer for the class discussion and described the importance of parental support of reading instruction. She also spent time reviewing the previous lecture on spoken language (including phonology), an important Previewing activity that would connect the current topic to the previous one while activating the students' prior knowledge. (The instructor also reminded her students of an upcoming lesson—connecting West African and contemporary language.)

The instructor reviewed the previous lesson on spoken language by asking students to name one component of language (e.g., syntax, morphology). A sample of her follow-up questioning techniques included, "Is rock a bound or unbound morpheme?"—very effective. Students, after answering, picked a number between one and twenty to signify who would be questioned next.

As the instructor introduced key terms (e.g., paired association), she provided the definitions as part of the dialogue, which modeled the "definition context clue" that is so prevalent in vocabulary reading instruction. She did an excellent job of making eye contact with her students. She modulated her speech for affect, and grounded her lecture in the use of overhead graphics without regurgitating them word for word. She had an engaging speaking style that facilitated the attention of her students. During the lecture, she engaged in dialogue with her students as a way of checking for understanding, another critical feature of effective instruction. By modeling these features, she provides a very effective connection to her lectures and effective teaching in the school classroom.

As always, it is an honor to sit in on a class led by a RFTEN faculty member. The instructor did a very effective job of relating critical information using a nice presentation style. It was obvious that her lectures incorporated information covered in RFTEN professional development activities.

The EDU 2200 class—Introduction to the Teaching of Reading was observed. The RFTEN faculty member, and the associate professor of education discussed both formative and summative assessments with her class. She began the class period by finding out what the students already knew about reading assessments and then built upon their background of knowledge by introducing other forms of informal assessment. The last half of the period she shared procedures for administering the TPRI (Texas Primary Reading Inventory).

At the end of each semester, students completed surveys to examine what new information they had learned. Statistical analyses by the program evaluation staff found that in all areas surveyed, students had gained knowledge about reading and how it is taught. The gains were not only statistically significant but of such a magnitude that they could also be considered meaningfully different.

Collegial Assistance

Throughout the RFTEN project, members discussed the need to interact with colleagues at their institutions and in the community so they could share what they learned through RFTEN. Within institutions, such collaboration is vital, because seldom does one faculty member teach all reading courses offered by a department. By sharing RFTEN materials and strategies, instructors can "spread the wealth" among their colleagues to ensure that students in all classes receive consistent, research-based information.

It is also important for institutional faculty to share information with educators in their surrounding areas. By sharing project information with principals and teachers, faculty members can influence classroom practices, which ensures that student teachers and interns are able to practice SBRR-related teaching methods. Consultant comments reflect such collaboration among colleagues:

> After the meeting with Dean Jeter, I met with a group of instructors from the education department. This group consisted of a RFTEN member who teaches Reading and Language Arts methods courses, an instructor from the Early Childhood faculty, a professor who teaches social studies methods courses, multicultural education courses, and foundations courses, a professor who teaches reading courses, and a public school reading teacher in the Wilberforce, Ohio, area.

> The foregoing meeting lasted until noon. I began by sharing with the group about RFTEN, specifically touching on each of the five big ideas: the development of phonemic awareness, phonics—word study, vocabulary, reading fluency, and comprehension. Specifically, I addressed scientifically based methods and current materials that have been used effectively to develop children's reading and writing abilities. We then discussed specific needs shared by the instructors. One of the main areas of discussion

included ways to improve and diversify the language of their learners. Within their student body were many young people studying to be teacher educators whose dialect and language patterns differed from traditional language patterns. This conversation was both enlightening and stimulating. I was able to share vocabulary development ideas as well as ideas for developing fluency. I brought copies of the Texas Online Learning Academies and was able to share with the group how the demonstrations would help them. Dr. Latson then shared many of the materials she received while attending a RFTEN meeting in the Washington, DC, area. Dr. Latson said the RFTEN materials would be available to the other faculty in the teacher education program to help them incorporate literacy strategies within their content areas. We also spent time discussing public school–university partnerships and field experiences.

That evening, I presented a workshop to about 150 Madison Elementary School parents that focused on reading to their children. I spent considerable time discussing phonological awareness and provided a number of activities they could do with their children to help teach phonological awareness skills. I then modeled procedures for reading aloud, and the parents later practiced their new skills with their children under the supervision of Drs. Davis and Boger and their teacher candidates. This was an exciting event, one of three that were scheduled for the spring, to involve parents in their children's learning, especially as it pertained to early reading. Children were given photocopied books to read with their parents, and time was spent during these activities for parents and children to share the experience together. Obviously, many parents do not possess skills in oral reading nor have strategies for helping their children get the most from the experience. Workshops like this are designed to assist parents in this effort. It was exciting opportunity to help out.

The College of Education at Jackson State University, Jackson, Mississippi, in conjunction with the RFTEN project, sponsored its second annual conference on literacy in January 2007. As the RFTEN consultant to Jackson State, I was asked to speak during the conference. I conducted two sessions on reading assessment (with a focus on fluency), one in the morning and one in the afternoon.

Faculty at California State University–Northridge (CSUN) were welcoming, involved, and interested in learning about research and scientifically based reading instruction. They have incorporated SBRR into their classes and have utilized the knowledge and materials received through their involvement with the RFTEN project. The faculty self-study and the informative sessions for parents are the result of RFTEN initiatives. CSUN's self-study group meets regularly and includes faculty from several departments within the College of Education, including Educational Leadership. Graduate students were also invited. The collegiality displayed was largely due to the efforts of the RFTEN members, who shared SBRR with colleagues.

Dr. Wynne Schilling of York College–CUNY, Jamaica, New York, asked me to prepare a presentation on comprehension and strategies for instruction and assessment to a group of York student teachers and their supervising teachers who were meeting that afternoon. I created a PowerPoint presentation on instructional strategies for narrative and expository text and also focused on processes for monitoring student understanding and growth. I shared videos from OTRAs that showed different comprehension and progress monitoring strategies, and I prepared a packet for each member that included activities and handouts taken from the OTRAs and the SERP. I began by asking what strategies successful readers use and then asked the teachers to share the most critical issues they identified for their own students (word identification). I tried to focus the presentation based on their concerns.

Another way to effect change is to work with non-participating faculty members to share RFTEN project information that members' colleagues can incorporate into their coursework. This is vital to systems change, because participating teachers tend to constitute a minority of faculty representation in teacher preparation courses. In faculty surveys, some items reflected collegial collaboration. Instructor responses indicated that the vast majority of faculty members were either working with their fellow faculty members or planned to do so.

HEC Online

HEC Online served as a forum for instructors' discussion around topics they identified. It was also a holding place for electronic documents such as syllabi, handouts, and activities in a space called "Shared Documents." Instructors could interact with one another in discussions as well as through sharing of documents. HEC Online afforded opportunities to

1. Collaborate with colleagues. This is especially helpful for faculty in small institutions that have limited opportunities to connect with others in their field.
2. Build individual and institutional capacity.
3. Create a base of support for inclusion of SBRR in reading instruction at the classroom and college level.
4. Clarify.
5. Network—within and across institutions.
6. Receive a "pat on the back."
7. Sustain RFTEN activities post-grant. Once seminars end, the online community becomes a way for people to stay connected.

We also talked about HEC Online and the importance of accessing the service and posting information on a regular basis. Ms. Amiotte has accessed the site, but she feels that she needs to do so more frequently, and I agreed.

We also spent some time discussing the HEC Online and how Loye could use the service to share information about her efforts as well as solicit information from her RFTEN colleagues. We spent some time exploring the texasreading.org website for free downloads, which could supplement her existing materials nicely. As usual, I spent time discussing the Academies and the Struggling Readers Institute materials and how information contained on the compact disks could benefit her students. We also spent considerable time discussing how to use assessment data to inform instruction.

The subject of textbooks came up, and I explained to them that I could not recommend textbooks because we were federally funded. I mentioned that HEC Online is a good place to get ideas for such matters.

We also talked about HEC Online and the importance of accessing the service and posting information on a regular basis. Both instructors had accessed the site, but they felt that they need to do so more frequently, and I agreed.

We discussed the importance of the HEC Online and posting information periodically. Kellee shared that she had gone online and posted information about the symposium, and I congratulated her on doing so. I explained that it is important for others to see successful efforts for spreading Reading First–related information and stated that others, hopefully, would be able to replicate her efforts.

Throughout the project, instructors were asked about the utility of HEC Online. The program evaluation data and the comments made by members suggest that HEC Online had potential for sharing and learning that was utilized by some, but not as many as hoped. Although some participants were frequent visitors who posted regularly on a variety of topics, others rarely accessed the service, whether they had problems logging in or simply had no interest.

SBRR Integration

SBRR has been a cornerstone of the RFTEN project, which is based on the No Child Left Behind Act. SBRR has five major considerations:

1. It applies rigorous, systematic, and objective procedures to obtain valid knowledge relevant to reading development, reading instruction, and reading difficulties.
2. It employs systematic, empirical methods that draw on observation or experiment.
3. It involves rigorous data analysis that is adequate to test the stated hypothesis and justify the general conclusions drawn.
4. It relies on measurements or observational methods that provide valid

data across evaluators and observers and across multiple measurements and observations.

5. It has been accepted by a peer-reviewed journal or approved by a panel of independent experts through a comparably rigorous, objective, and scientific review.

More important than what SBRR is, however, is what it means to participating RFTEN institutions and their reading programs. For RFTEN, SBRR means that only reading approaches that pass rigorous standards of research will be taught to students who will one day be reading teachers. Educational history is replete with approaches to reading instruction that have come and gone. Others have withstood the test of time even though there is no credible research support for the technique. Thus, reading teachers have been taught how to teach reading using questionable and faulty methods and materials. Many students who are taught using these non-research-based methods never learn how to read, and the RFTEN project's adherence to SBRR is designed to see that such faulty teaching no longer occurs.

Mrs. Thornton consistently integrates research with the required coursework. She demonstrated this by showing me the articles that her students read and the reflective papers that they wrote. These articles are all placed online for students to download.

Three instructors discussed the ways they have integrated the knowledge and materials they have received through RFTEN. They have incorporated SBRR into student lessons and assignments and have used the *Put Reading First* booklet and the 3 Tier Reading model materials. They concentrated on teaching the five essential components of reading; their candidates have commented that the RFTEN materials have enhanced their knowledge, skills, and confidence regarding the teaching of reading.

The Livingstone (University, Salisbury, North Carolina) Reading First room is a wonderful example of using RFTEN resources effectively. In the room, which also serves as a classroom, are a variety of reading texts (e.g., patterned texts, early readers), posters, textbooks, and other materials that have been purchased with RFTEN monies. Students can see how SBRR is translated into practice and can obtain hands-on experiences with materials that have been proven to be effective.

The program evaluation leads toward the conclusion that RFTEN has changed the system at participating institutions with regard to the way students are taught to teach reading. Syllabi have been changed to reflect SBRR, RFTEN participants are learning more about SBRR and related interventions and are teaching what they know to students, students are learning and applying SBRR-related concepts, and RFTEN members are sharing their knowledge with other professionals in their community (i.e., institution colleagues and public school personnel). Change has already taken place. If the old adage holds true that the best predictor of future performance is existing performance, members are affecting practice that will endure past the current funding cycle.

Field Placements

Field placements occur throughout a student teacher's education. Early on, students are placed in classrooms to see teachers in action and schoolchildren learn. Later, internships and practicum experiences allow college and university students to gain hands-on experience teaching children. Finally, students spend a semester to a year doing their student teaching, where they begin to take responsibility for teaching and managing an entire classroom.

Field placements allow consultants to see how classroom instruction is being applied. Do supervising teachers use SBRR-related techniques? Do they teach each of the five areas of reading? Do they teach using systematic, explicit instructional techniques? Or do they teach reading implicitly? How are assessments given, and how are the test data interpreted? By sitting in classrooms and observing student teachers in action, consultants can gauge the extent to which what is being taught at the college and university is actually being implemented by the student teachers as they practice teaching.

Preservice teachers work in the local Reading First schools.

I also spent some time with Dr. McGowan and Mrs. Williams (Alcorn State University, Lorman, Mississippi) to answer a question they had about integrating student teacher and intern placements with RFTEN goals and objectives (i.e., to help ensure that their students apply the skills they learn in class). I congratulated them on recognizing the importance of having their students apply the skills they are learning in class to actual interactions with students. I also mentioned the importance of providing students with opportunities to interact with parents so that parents can support their children's reading. I shared the work instructors are doing at North Carolina Agricultural and Technical State University, Greensboro, North Carolina (with Madison Elementary School), and they shared with me some of their programs and how they might be modified to include more face-to-face interactions between Alcorn students and parents. For instance, they have a tutoring program wherein the students meet with parents at the end of the program to discuss what they did and share assessment results. We identified this as an excellent opportunity to expand the contact with teachers to include strategies that parents can use at home to support what was being done during the tutoring sessions.

Another issue that came up during the discussion is the perceived disconnection between what teacher candidates are being taught and what they are being asked to do in the classroom. Teacher candidates at Kean University, Union, New Jersey, are taught to actively engage students in learning and then when they get to their field placement they are handed "scripts" and worksheets to use with the students. Partly because of this, there is concern that there are not enough good mentor teachers/settings for the number of field placements the institution requires (about a thousand per semester).

We discussed Kean's students and the field experiences they are offered. We spoke of the selection of schools and their cooperating teachers. It was apparent that many of the teachers are using instructional practices that reflect Reading First–endorsed practices.

The Alcorn State team shared with me information about the clinical practicum in Reading (EDCI 5210). This is a graduate-level course where candidates in the Reading Specialist Master's program must complete a clinical practicum work with two to four students at a time for a total of sixty contact hours. The students whom the Reading Specialist Master's program teachers teach have reading difficulties. This practicum takes place in the summer and is team taught by instructors in education and speech pathology.

The instructor also shared with me a special component to the clinical practicum in reading. Every Friday during the practicum, three graduate students work together to provide professional development to the other members of the practicum. The group presentations must address one of the five components of reading and provide information that will be useful to teachers and is relevant to the teaching process. <Participant> provided me with a CD that has video footage of all the group presentations. I viewed one presentation while at Xavier University, Cincinnati, Ohio, and observed two practicum teachers presenting information on phonemic awareness.

I first observed Mrs. H. (a practicum student teaching students during the summer) while visiting the Xavier Summer Reading Program teaching two girls who will enter the third grade in the fall. She began the day's lessons with a fluency-building activity that had a student reading Dolch sight words [the Dolch Word List is a list of commonly used English words that was originally compiled by Edward William Dolch, Ph.D.] (second grade) with fluency (i.e., quickly and accurately). I liked the fact that Mrs. H used a timer to help keep students on task and to ensure that her instruction was well paced and that there was more student work and less teacher talk.

Although knowledge cannot guarantee effective teaching, before one can teach effectively one must have knowledge about what and how to teach. Program evaluators examined the student survey data to determine student knowledge while the students were taking clinical courses. With rare exceptions, the data demonstrated that students in clinical classes gained knowledge of effective reading practices and learned how to apply SBRR in their clinical experiences.

To review the information in this report, RFTEN consultants worked with their participant colleagues in a variety of ways. Whether via e-mail or phone conversations or personal on-site visits, the consultants stressed the importance of teaching students effective, research-validated procedures for teaching reading. By focusing on the various aspects of the project (e.g., course syllabi, field experiences), consultants were able to share their expertise and provide reinforcement for skills learned during RFTEN-sponsored professional development activities. Each consultant came away from his or her visit acknowledging that RFTEN materials were being utilized and that faculty members were indeed applying what they had learned as part of the project.

I mentioned earlier that Mary McLeod Bethune founded Bethune-Cookman College. We can only hope that the goals set forth by Mrs. Bethune and others who helped found the RFTEN institutions will be fulfilled in part each time a child goes home from class taught by a teacher who attended an RFTEN institution and tells his or her family, "I can read!"

The Role of Quality Assurance Coaching Consultants

DENISE LITTLETON

AND CONTRIBUTING: MARGARET COLE WHITE

RFTEN sought and benefited from retired and practicing education faculty and administrators, reading and education experts, and those with experience working with the National Council for Accreditation of Teacher Education (NCATE) to support the development of an effective implementation and training project.

These fourteen consultants, known as Quality Assurance Coaching Consultants (QACCs), supported the integration of scientifically based reading research (SBRR) into teaching preparation curricula. QACCs were assigned to work with up to three RFTEN institutions. They supported these colleges and universities as well as the RFTEN project by

- assisting teacher education units to form effective teams to lead the implementation process
- coaching teacher education units to develop a vision for change that was achievable, challenging, long term, easy to grasp, vivid, and compelling
- assisting teacher education units to communicate clearly and collaboratively with all RFTEN stakeholders
- assisting teacher education units to remove barriers and provide incentives for those who are involved in the implementation of SBRR
- assisting teacher education units to revise performance-based assessment measures to reflect RFTEN project goals

To accomplish these tasks, the QACCs visited a total of thirty-eight participating RFTEN institutions, assisting administrators in formulating plans and implementing SBRR within the pre-kindergarten to sixth grade (PK–6) teacher education curriculum. Before QACCs visited a RFTEN campus, they received training, and they used a template designed by the project to guide their work on the campuses. These scheduled visits included meetings and interviews with the president, other senior-level campus administrators, faculty, and teacher candidates. To provide full support for their assigned RFTEN institutions, QACCs also reviewed relevant documents and visited local elementary schools to assess the campus/school collaboration. QACCs also used a needs assessment tool to help determine the institution's capacity to be successful in the RFTEN project and to implement change in the teacher preparation curriculum. After each visit to a RFTEN institution, QACCs wrote and submitted a comprehensive report to the project's national office. Those colleges and universities participating in RFTEN's Cohorts 1 and 2 received three site visits from their QACCs, and Cohort 3 institutions, which joined the RFTEN project in year three, received usually one but sometimes two site visits.

As former or current faculty and/or administrators of minority-serving institutions, the QACCs were sensitive to and cognizant of the management styles and organizational structures of these partner colleges and universities. They were able to provide support and suggestions that were informed by their experiences and work with these institutions.

For instance, QACCs interviewed and had access to key administrators responsible for making decisions on campus. In one situation, for the project to be successfully implemented, a faculty member with expertise in reading education needed to be employed. The dean had initiated conversations with the vice president for academic affairs to employ such a person, and the QACC supported this need in the interview with the vice president for academic affairs. As a former campus administrator and a reading educator, the QACC was familiar with the process and the budget requirements for new faculty positions and was able to articulate the benefits of employing a reading education faculty member. A common ground of experience between the QACC and the vice president for academic affairs led to productive discussions during site visits. When it came time for the next QACC visit (within two months), the dean was interviewing candidates for the position.

QACCs were also trained as coaches. Without being intrusive or critical, QACCs used coaching techniques to encourage faculty members and administrators to determine how the RFTEN project could be implemented on their campus to meet their specific needs. For example, QACCs used the following questions to generate discussions with faculty: "What do you want to accomplish with this project on your campus?" or "How can this project best meet your local needs?" Such queries were designed to help faculty foster a vision of how the RFTEN project could be implemented and made uniquely their own. What resulted were creative and effective—yet diverse—models of project implementation among the institutions.

Gathering Data from Site Visit 1: Assessing Project Readiness

Toward the end of the project's second year, RFTEN enlisted fourteen external evaluators, who were university researchers and scholars. The evaluators reflected the racial and ethnic diversity of the RFTEN institutions (black, Hispanic, and Native American). Their charge was to review and rate site visit reports the QACCs produced. A framework template and rubric were used to guide the work of the external evaluators. The reports submitted by QACCs after site visits in year one varied in format, which made it challenging for these evaluators and for the RFTEN staff to extract the data needed to determine an institution's readiness.

Six questions guided the QACCs' interviewing and reporting process during the first site visit:

1. What is the status of the institutional/administrative support for SBRR at the participating institution?
2. Had the administration established a learning community within the unit by collaborating with faculty responsible for teacher candidates' learning?
3. What provisions were made to sustain the training of preservice candidates in reading?
4. To what extent does a plan exist for extending SBRR training to other faculty members within the school/department/college of education (SDC) who are responsible for preparing preservice teachers?
5. What assessment system existed for evaluating courses, programs, and clinical experiences?
6. To what extent is teacher candidate licensure data maintained and how are the data used to evaluate and improve programs?

These six questions also guided the external evaluators' review of the QACCs' reports. Table 1 lists the rubric and template used to rate each report and determine each institution's readiness to begin the RFTEN project.

The format for the rubric is similar to the format used by NCATE for its standards. There are three ratings: (1) unacceptable, (2) acceptable, and (3) target. The focus of the first site visit was the institution's readiness to begin the process of implementing SBRR.

Table 1. Rubric for Site Visit 1: 2003–2004, RFTEN Year 1

Categories / Questions Criteria	Unacceptable Report fails to provide evidence for this category.	Acceptable Report provides adequate evidence for this category.	Target Report provides substantive evidence for this category.
Administration support for ongoing professional development	The president's or provost's support cannot be ascertained. No evidence the president or designee attended RFTEN meetings for presidents. Little or no participation by the dean is noted. No evidence of scheduled meetings and release time for faculty. Instructional materials to support SBRR are not evident. Little support is provided on-campus for SBRR professional development within the unit.	The president/provost is aware and supportive of the project. The president/designee or dean is responsible for monitoring and implementation of the project. The president's designee or dean attended RFTEN meetings. The president's designee or dean supports a climate for collaboration through the following: release time for faculty for scheduled meetings within the unit to engage in systemic knowledge building about SBRR; and instructional materials to support SBRR.	The president/provost is engaged actively in the project, discusses the scope of the project and the degree to which SBRR is being implemented at his/her institution. The president's designee or dean attended all RFTEN meetings for presidents. The president's designee or dean develops/leads a climate for collaboration through the following: release time for faculty for scheduled meetings both on- and off-campus to engage in systemic knowledge building about SBRR; and instructional materials to support SBRR.
Administration establishes a learning community	Limited evidence of collaboration among faculty within the unit who are responsible for teacher candidates' learning. Limited collaboration with the arts and sciences and the professional P-12 community exists.	The president/designee or dean is responsible for implementing a learning community within the unit's conceptual framework. There is evidence of collaboration among faculty within the unit who are responsible for teacher candidates' learning. There is evidence of review of student practice/research to improve student learning. The learning community extends through the arts and sciences.	The president/designee or dean is responsible for implementing a learning community within the unit's conceptual framework. There is evidence of collaboration among unit faculty, arts and sciences faculty, and P-12 practitioners to prepare teacher candidates' learning to improve student learning.

Sustainability for the training of candidates	There is limited evidence of a plan and/or documents to sustain the training of preservice candidates in the area of reading. The RFTEN faculty representative has not revised course syllabi with feedback from the Vaughn Gross Center for Reading and Language Arts, University of Texas, Austin (VGCRLA) reading consultant. Field and clinical experiences are not carried out in school environments that incorporate an SBRR approach. Partnering with a Reading First school is not included in the plan.	There is evidence of a plan and/or documents to sustain the training of preservice candidates in the area of reading. The RFTEN faculty representative has revised course syllabi with feedback from the VGCRLA reading consultant. Selected field and clinical experiences are carried out in school environments that incorporate an SBRR approach. Partnering with a Reading First school is included in the plan.	Documents provide evidence of change to sustain the training of preservice candidates in the area of reading. The RFTEN faculty representative and other reading faculty have revised course syllabi with feedback from the VGCRLA reading consultant. Field and clinical experiences are carried out in school environments that incorporate an SBRR approach. Partnering with a Reading First school is included in the plan. Position announcements contain notation of expectation that new faculty have knowledge of SBRR.
Plan for extending SBRR training to other faculty	There is no evidence of a plan for extending SBRR training to other faculty within the school of education (SOE) who are responsible for the preparation of preservice teachers.	There is evidence of a plan with timelines for extending SBRR training to other faculty within the SOE who are responsible for the preparation of preservice teacher candidates. The RFTEN faculty representative has provided professional development from participation with the VGCRLA reading consultant.	The plan with timelines provides for extending SBRR training to all faculty within the SOE who are responsible for the preparation of preservice teacher candidates. Selected arts and sciences faculty and public school clinical faculty are included in the plan. The RFTEN faculty representative has provided professional development from participation with the VGCRLA reading consultant.

Table continued from previous page.

Categories / Questions Criteria	Unacceptable	Acceptable	Target
	Report fails to provide evidence for this category.	Report provides adequate evidence for this category.	Report provides substantive evidence for this category.
Assessment system	There is limited or no evidence that an integrated system exists for evaluating courses, clinical experiences, and programs. Program changes made within the past three years within the unit are not documented within the assessment system and program minutes.	There is evidence that an integrated system exists for evaluating courses, clinical experiences, and programs at critical decision points. Both candidate and faculty performance are reviewed regularly with a goal of improving candidate learning outcomes. Program changes made within the past three years within the unit are documented within the assessment system and program minutes.	There is evidence that an integrated system exists for evaluating courses, clinical experiences, and programs at critical decision points. Candidate and faculty performance include self- and other-assessment that are reviewed regularly with a goal of improving candidate and student learning outcomes. Program changes made within the past three years within the unit are documented within the assessment system and program minutes.
Teacher candidate licensure data	There is limited documentation that teacher candidate licensure data are maintained for program, state, and national publics for gauging candidate proficiency.	There is evidence of documentation that teacher candidate licensure data are maintained for program, state, and national publics for gauging candidate proficiency. These data are used to measure progress of candidates and aggregated to evaluate and improve programs.	There is evidence of documentation that teacher candidate licensure data are maintained for program, state, and national publics for gauging candidate proficiency. Follow-up data are collected from employers. These data are used to measure progress of candidates and aggregated to evaluate and improve programs.

After using the rubric to evaluate each report, the evaluators' final evaluations for each institution were submitted using the template given in Table 2.

Table 2. Assessment Form for Evaluating RFTEN Site Reports

SITE REPORT EVALUATION FORM

Second and Third Visits
Please use this form in conjunction with the appropriate rubric to assess the RFTEN site reports that you have been assigned. The purpose of the review is to evaluate the quality of the reports by assigning a numerical score and relevant comments.

Name of Reviewer:
Institutional Affiliation:
Institutional Report That is Being Reviewed:
Year of the Institutional Report: ___Spring '04 ___Fall '04 ___Spring '05

---

1. Institutional/Administrative Support for SBRR
Evaluate the status of the institutional/administrative support for SBRR at the participating RFTEN institution. What evidence is or is not revealed to demonstrate the involvement of the administration?
Comments:

2. Degree of the SBRR Implementation in the Institution's Reading Program
Evaluate the status of the degree of SBRR implementation in the institution's reading program. What evidence is or is not revealed to demonstrate these efforts?
Comments:

3. Using Available Resources
Evaluate the status of the use of available resources at the participating RFTEN institution. What evidence is or is not revealed to demonstrate these efforts?
Comments:

4. Candidates' Opportunity to Practice SBRR in Real Classrooms
Evaluate the level of opportunities that teacher candidates have to practice SBRR in real classroom settings. What evidence is or is not revealed to demonstrate these efforts?
Comments:

5. Degree of Institutional Change
Evaluate the level of institutional change that the participating RFTEN institution has undergone since the implementation of RFTEN? What evidence is or is not revealed to demonstrate these efforts?
Comments:

6. Institutionalization (For Third Site Visit Only)
Evaluate the level of institutional capacity that the participating institution has undergone since the implementation of RFTEN. What evidence is or is not revealed to demonstrate these efforts?
Comments:

Summary of the Findings from the Quality of Site Report

Directions: In light of your assessment of the various categories within the rubric, please provide a summary of the overall quality of the site report for which you have evaluated. Your summary should highlight the categories in which were identified in the rubric.

In addition, please identify any recurring themes that your analysis has revealed as well as any other significant findings. Please provide a minimum of 5 paragraphs.

A rating of 1 stands for an unacceptable rating, 2 stands for an acceptable rating, and 3 stands for a target rating for each category. For example, to be on target for administrative support, the description stated (see Table 1), "The president or provost is actively engaged in the project, discusses the scope of the project and the degree to which SBRR is being implemented in his/her institution. The president's designee or dean attended all meetings for presidents. The president's designee or dean develops/leads a climate for collaboration through the following: release time for faculty for scheduled meetings both on and off campus to engage in systemic knowledge building about SBRR and provides funds to purchase instructional materials to support SBRR." If the QACCs' report provided evidence to satisfy this rubric, the institution was given a rating of 3. That value was then recorded on the evaluation template (Table 2). Each category was reviewed and rated.

It is important to note that in the initial phase of the RFTEN project, at least two of the selected institutions were determined not to be ready to participate in the project and withdrew. Remaining were the colleges and universities that were ready to implement the project and were committed to RFTEN's goals and mission.

In what follows, I provide a summary of how the external evaluators rated the RFTEN institutions based on the five questions.

Institutional support

During the first site visit only 15 percent of the institutions were rated unacceptable, and 85 percent were rated acceptable and above in the category of institutional support. For the project to be instituted on the campus, presidents and vice presidents signed an agreement indicating their support. Therefore it was surprising that some institutions were rated unacceptable in this category. There were many examples of strong institutional support. Twenty-two presidents from partner institutions attended the RFTEN national meeting and became active members of the RFTEN president's advisory board.

In other examples, an RFTEN faculty member at an institution was given release time or a reduced course load to support the operation of the project; the RFTEN coordinator was given office space to manage the project; and one president authorized the establishment of a Reading First curriculum laboratory. In addition, some campus presidents became so engaged in the RFTEN project that they requested written reports about how RFTEN was progressing and being implemented in their unit and on campus. They were also actively engaged in and supportive of RFTEN-sponsored training and national reading and education conferences.

Learning community

Establishing a learning community, if one did not exist, was important to this project. Again, 85 percent of the RFTEN institutions presented evidence that learning communities existed or were being developed. Cross-program teaching occurred in some institutions. Speech language pathologists and English faculty members were sharing expertise in professional education classes in the area of phonology and using sentence structure or syntax to enhance comprehension. Several faculty members from different program areas team-taught a course. There were instances of professional development schools and partnerships existing or being developed with several public schools and school districts. Plans for reading faculty to share information with each other and with other liberal arts faculty regularly were in the works.

Training preservice teachers

For this category, QACCs looked for evidence that would show definite or planned changes in the curriculum to incorporate SBRR. Seventy-four percent of the institutions demonstrated a focus on training preservice teachers in SBRR. This training was reflected in curriculum content, revised syllabi, clinical experiences in the public schools, and the addition of reading courses that incorporated evidence-based reading instruction.

Extending training to other faculty

RFTEN faculty were encouraged to share the training and resources they received with other schools, departments, and colleges of education (SCDE) faculty on their campuses. It was this category that the QACCs' knowledge of how campuses functioned proved valuable. QACCs were able to provide support and encouragement to the RFTEN faculty while encouraging deans or department heads to provide opportunities for RFTEN faculty members to share their SBRR training with other faculty members. To accomplish this, many QACCs assisted administrators in developing a timeline for extending SBRR training to other faculty. It was also in this category that 52 percent of the institutions were rated unacceptable on the first site visit.

Assessment system

According to QACCs, the majority (89 percent) of institutions presented evidence of an integrated system for evaluating courses, clinical experiences, and programs.

Sources of data included surveys, practicum/internship/student teaching evaluations, departmental tests, faculty evaluations, state process reviews, and employer satisfaction data. In addition, preliminary assessment systems to determine candidates' impact upon PK–6 student learning were underway.

Data use for improving programs

Multiple data sources that looked at teacher licensure and teacher candidates were used to evaluate and improve programs. State data and employment data from school systems were routinely reviewed and used to improve programs. In many states such data were public. The data also provided incentives for institutions to maintain or enhance programs to improve not only state ratings but also the public's perception of the institution. In this category, 82 percent of the institutions were rated acceptable or above.

Gathering Data from Site Visits 2 and 3: Assessing Project Implementation and Sustainability

QACCs, on their second and third campus site visits, sought answers to five questions:

1. What is the status of the institutional/administrative support for SBRR at the participating institutions?
2. What is the degree of SBRR implementation in the institution's reading program?
3. To what extent are institutions using available resources?
4. To what extent do candidates have the opportunity to practice in real classrooms?
5. What was the degree of institutional change?

The following question on the institutionalization of the RFTEN project was added during the third (last) site visit: "What is the level of institutional capacity or commitment to support SBRR beyond the project's duration?" The rubric outlined in Table 3 was used to evaluate QACCs' reports. The external evaluators recorded their ratings on a similar template to the one used for the first site visit, incorporating the second set of questions.

Table 3. Rubric for Site Visits 2 and 3

Categories/Questions Criteria	Unacceptable	Acceptable	Target
	Report fails to provide evidence for this category.	Report provides adequate evidence for this category.	Report provides substantive evidence for this category.
Institutional/administrative support for SBRR	The president's or provost's support cannot be ascertained. No evidence the president or designee attended RFTEN meetings for presidents. Little or no mention of the dean's role is noted. No evidence of collaboration between SBRR-trained faculty, other faculty members, and the VGCRLA reading consultant.	The president or provost is supportive and clearly aware of the project. The president's designee or dean is directly responsible for the monitoring and implementation of the project. President or designee attended RFTEN meetings. Evidence of collaboration among RFTEN faculty, other faculty members and VGCRLA reading consultant.	The president/provost is engaged actively in the project, discusses the scope of the project and the degree to which SBRR is being implemented at his/her institution. President attended all RFTEN meetings for presidents. The dean is actively involved and may be the catalyst for the project. The VGCRLA reading consultant has been on site and has participated with RFTEN faculty and other faculty members in the planning or implementation of professional development workshops.
Degree of SBRR implementation in the institution's reading program	There is limited or no evidence indicating the revision of course syllabi or contact with the VGCRLA reading consultant by the RFTEN faculty representative. Minimal information regarding candidates' training in SBRR or exposure to the SBRR model.	The RFTEN faculty representative has revised course syllabi with feedback from the VGCRLA reading consultant. Evidence of SBRR implementation is noted in candidates' lesson plans, test results, in-class teaching demonstrations, portfolios, etc.	Course syllabi have been revised with continual feedback and communication with VGCRLA reading consultant. Key faculty members have attended RFTEN Collaborative Seminars. VGCRLA reading consultants have made site visits and provided training to university faculty, public school faculty, and/or students. Evidence of SBRR implementation is noted in candidates' lesson plans, test results, in-class teaching demonstrations, portfolios, etc.

Using available resources	There is no mention of using the following available: resources: • RFTEN website; • HEC online; • seminars and workshops; • RFTEN staff • RFTEN faculty at other institutions.	Use of some of the following resources are mentioned: RFTEN website; HEC online; seminars and workshops; RFTEN staff; RFTEN faculty at other institutions.	There is evidence the site has used most of the available resources identified and has shared information by posting information on the website, submitted a publication for the RFTEN staff for support and ideas for expanding the program.
Candidates' opportunity to practice SBRR in real classrooms	Partnership with a Reading First school or another appropriate school is not evident. There is limited or no mention of opportunities for candidates to practice SBRR.	Partnership with a Reading First school or another appropriate school is evident. Candidates are provided opportunities to practice SBRR in selected clinical experiences.	There is evidence of a strong collaborative relationship with a Reading First school or another public school. Evidence of candidates' opportunity to practice SBRR is reflected throughout the curriculum in Level 1, 2, and 3 clinical experiences. Candidates are evaluated and provided support for implementing SBRR by their cooperating teacher and university supervisor in a Reading First or another appropriate school.
Degree of institutional change	Little evidence is provided documenting institutional change. Revision of course syllabi, VGCRLA support, faculty development seminars, curriculum changes, and documentation of candidates' knowledge are not discussed.	Some evidence is provided documenting institutional change. Examples include revision of course syllabi, attendance at RFTEN Collaborative Seminars, collaboration with other institutional faculty members, planning and offering professional development seminars, and candidates' knowledge and use of SBRR.	The "majority of the indicators listed under the "acceptable" category are included. In addition there is evidence that specific assessments, surveys, questionnaires, and/or pilot studies have been developed to evaluate curriculum changes, candidates' knowledge, and candidates' impact upon PK–6 student learning.

Table continued from previous page.

Categories/Questions	Unacceptable	Acceptable	Target
Criteria	Report fails to provide evidence for this category.	Report provides adequate evidence for this category.	Report provides substantive evidence for this category.
Institutionalization (third site visit only)	There is no evidence of institutional capacity or commitment to support SBRR beyond the project's duration.	Administrative and faculty commitment are evident. SBRR has been embraced particularly by the reading faculty and most likely will continue beyond the funding period. Institutional capacity is noted.	Most of the structures put into place (i.e., faculty development seminars, curriculum changes, and revision of course syllabi) to support SBRR will most likely remain. Reading and other faculty members have embraced SBRR. There is indication of institutional capacity, a strong commitment, and administrative support to continue beyond the scope and support of the project.
Total			

Note: This rubric is designed to assist reviewers in determining whether the report from the on-site visit addressed the project questions.

The following discussion summarizes how the external evaluators rated each category.

Institutional support

The first question focused on the status of the institutional administrative support for SBRR implementation. For site visit 2, four institutions had an unacceptable rating. By the third visit, however, only two institutions had an unacceptable rating. The reduction signaled the evolution of RFTEN on those campuses. The site visit reports also found that RFTEN's visibility on the campuses had increased by the second and third visits and was tied to the support of the administration. At one institution, for example, the president nominated the RFTEN faculty and project for local, state, and national awards. The institution won these awards and received certificates, honors, and recognition by the city, the state legislature, and the federal government. At another institution, the vice president shared RFTEN activities campuswide by placing them on the university's calendar. Many site visit reports also reflected evidence of additional full-time and adjunct faculty being hired to teach reading. Finally, at another institution, the president established a campuswide committee on reading and literacy and appointed the chair of the Department of Education its chair. The committee had a threefold charge: (1) to reduce the rate of illiteracy through community outreach, (2) to provide opportunities for those who were illiterate, and (3) to prepare teachers as instructional leaders in the area of reading in the public schools.

Implementing SBRR

The degree of SBRR implementation was a major focus for the QACCs during the second and third site visits. By the third site visit, 89 percent of the institutions were at an acceptable level or above. Teacher candidates from RFTEN institutions were placed in local Reading First schools, low-performing schools, and hard-to-staff schools, working with students in grades P–6. Core syllabi were revised. Reading consultants from the VGCRLA visited the campuses and provided training to the university faculty, public schools faculty, and students. SBRR implementation was reflected and included in the candidates' lesson plans and portfolios.

Available resources

The second site visit focused on the availability and use of resources at the institutions. Six RFTEN institutions out of twenty-four received an unacceptable rating, which meant that reading faculty, as well as the education faculty, were not familiar with and had not used any of the resources provided through the project. These resources included the RFTEN Web site (www.RFTEN.org), instructional materials, Higher Education Cooperative (HEC) Online, and teaching academy materials. By the third site visit, however, 89 percent of institutions, or sixteen out of eighteen, reported using those resources. Only two institutions had not. There were twenty-four and eighteen institutions, respectively, during site visits two and three. Also, information had been shared by faculty through RFTEN conference presentations, published articles, and newsletters or journals.

Practicing SBRR in real classrooms

To what extent were candidates provided opportunities to practice SBRR in real classrooms? By the third site visit, 89 percent of the institutions had earned an acceptable rating or above, and the difference between site visits two and three was negligible. There were many opportunities for candidates to use SBRR with children even in nontraditional classroom settings. Twenty institutions used observation and participation experiences for candidates to practice using SBRR while being observed by classroom teachers and/or university professors. Service learning opportunities were also used. Pull-out and after-school programs, as well as year-long internships, took place. Moreover, journals, lesson plans, portfolios, videos, photos, and student achievement data all documented the candidates' experience in working with P–6 students.

Institutional change

By the third site visit, institutional change was well underway, according to the site visit reports. Eighty-four percent of the institutions were rated at the acceptable level or above by the third visit. There was an increased focus on SBRR in the undergraduate teacher preparation curriculum and on P–6 student achievement. Not only were the institutions beginning to incorporate SBRR into the classroom, but there was an emphasis on candidates being aware of the impact of instruction on student achievement. Other examples included offering on-campus faculty development workshops and seminars, revising course syllabi to include relevant assignments incorporating SBRR, and initiating research studies to determine candidates' impact on classroom learning and P–6 student achievement after SBRR instruction.

Administrators hired reading faculty with terminal degrees in reading and provided support to faculty seeking a reading specialist qualification. At one institution, faculty members were given the opportunity to be retrained and/or to earn master's degrees in reading. At another RFTEN institution, faculty members from the schools of liberal arts and sciences were involved in the RFTEN project. Many schools developed centers of reading. Whether or not they called these RFTEN centers, reading centers, or early childhood centers, institutions began to develop such facilities to support professional development and to house materials for students, families, and communities.

RFTEN faculty, using a train-the-trainer model, often provided workshops for classroom teachers. In one instance, a P–6 program was implemented that challenged students to read 10,000 books. Institutions began to evaluate their assessment systems, and several institutions made changes in the unit's assessment system to incorporate the emphasis on reading. Another institution hired an assistant dean of assessment to develop a systemic program to evaluate the effectiveness of its teacher education program, the RFTEN project, candidate performance, and P–6 student achievement.

RFTEN faculty coordinated with state departments of education on Reading First initiatives. For example, one institution revised a degree it offered to include an emphasis on reading for its teacher candidates at the elementary level, and many adopted new textbooks and curriculum materials to support SBRR.

Institutionalization

The third site visit required QACCs to determine whether the RFTEN model at the partner colleges and universities could be extended or supported beyond the end of the national initiative and grant period. Eighty-six percent of institutions provided evidence of their ability to move forward.

Reading and literacy resource centers were established or enhanced to support university and classroom teachers, candidates, students, and the community. According to the QACCs, these centers were well established and not likely to be terminated once the RFTEN project concluded. New faculty members were hired in tenure-track positions and junior faculty were retooled to strengthen the program. New reading programs and courses were developed and existing ones were revised. Concentrations in literacy were offered for candidates seeking licensure in elementary education and those on the middle school levels, which reflected strong collaborations with liberal arts and arts faculty.

In areas where there was ample evidence of institutional support, there was also evidence of institutional modeling by administrators, particularly those who had considerable expertise in reading. Campus/school collaborations that existed were strengthened, and promising new partnerships were emerging. Further evidence of how RFTEN institutions planned to institutionalize their work was also found in the conceptual framework.

Summary of the Analysis of the External Evaluators' Ratings

RFTEN site visit reports were evaluated and analyzed after QACCs conducted three campus visits to thirty-one colleges and universities in the project. After a year and a half, the site visit reports were evaluated and analyzed. Seven institutions were evaluated in the third year and were not included in the external evaluators' review, which can be summarized as follows.

1. What is the status of the institutional/administrative support for SBRR at the participating institution?

Administrative support increased from 84 percent to 89 percent by the third site visit, with only two institutions rated as unsatisfactory in this category. Twenty-two university presidents attended a national meeting of the project and served as members of the project's advisory board; the dean was allowed to hire faculty members with expertise in reading education, and a president nominated the project on its campus for national and state awards.

2. Had the administration established a learning community within the unit by collaborating with faculty responsible for teacher candidates' learning?

QACCs reported cross-program teaching of several faculty members in two institutions. Either a speech pathologist provided coursework on phonology to prospective teachers or several faculty members team-taught a course. In many situations collaboration existed with faculty members inside and outside SDCEs. Eighty-five percent of the institutions were rated acceptable or above on this criterion.

3. What provisions were made to sustain the training of preservice candidates in reading?

By the first site visit, 74 percent of the institutions posted revised course syllabi including components of phonemic awareness, phonics, fluency, vocabulary development, and text comprehension. Additional reading courses were developed, and the curriculum content was revised. Faculty members had begun to identify and acquire state-of-the-art technology resources and materials to support SBRR. (See also question 10.)

4. To what extent does a plan exist for extending SBRR training to other faculty members within the SDCEs who are responsible for the preparation of preservice teachers?

Evidence for this was observed during the first site visit, with 48 percent of the institutions demonstrating that some faculty development in SBRR was occurring. The reading content consultants had provided training to other education faculty, college of liberal arts faculty, and public school faculty. Anecdotal records suggest this increased by the QACCs' third site visit.

5. What assessment system existed for evaluating courses, programs, and clinical experiences?

Several documents indicated that an assessment system existed for evaluating courses, programs, and clinical experiences in 89 percent of the participating institutions. In many instances, the assessment system was being revised to include candidates' knowledge in reading education. Sources of data included surveys, internship/student teacher evaluation, lesson plan evaluations, work samples, portfolios, examinations, and employer satisfaction data.

6. To what extent are teacher candidate licensure data maintained and how are the data used to evaluate and improve programs?

Eighty-two percent of the participating institutions documented that teacher licensure data were maintained and used to evaluate and improve programs. Program improvement data were collected at different intervals by internal assessments, external surveys, accrediting agencies, and state officials. Consultants were used periodically to evaluate programs and to provide comments to advisory groups and employers. Assessment data were used to improve programs at least each semester or annually.

7. What was the degree of SBRR implementation in the institution's reading program?

By the third site visit, only two institutions were rated unacceptable in this category. Course syllabi had been revised, and further evidence of SBRR implementation was noted in candidates' lesson plans, test results, portfolios, in-class teaching demonstrations, and student teaching/internship experiences. Reading faculty met regularly at several institutions to discuss the content of reading courses, in-service opportunities were provided for P–12 faculty, and workshop sessions were sponsored for parents.

8. To what extent are institutions using available resources?

Eighty-nine percent of the institutions used the available resources at the acceptable level or better by the third site visit. At the highest level, all of the resources provided by the project were utilized, and many academicians shared information through conference presentations, published articles, and communication with other institutions.

9. To what extent do candidates have the opportunity to practice in real classrooms?

Reading First schools, professional development schools, low-performing schools, and partnership schools on the elementary level collaborated with the participating institutions to provide real classrooms for candidates to practice SBRR. Eighty-nine percent of the institutions met this criterion at the acceptable level or better.

10. What was the degree of institutional change?

Institutional change varied according to an institution's use of SBRR at the beginning of the project. Yet examples of institutional change ranged from an increased focus on the five components of SBRR in reading courses to a complete revision of reading education curriculum provided for teacher candidates. A degree program was revised to include an endorsement in reading education for teacher candidates at the elementary level, and an assessment system was changed to measure candidates' knowledge to teach reading. Eighty-four percent of the institutions reflected a degree of institutional change at an acceptable level or better.

11. What is the level of institutional capacity or commitment to support SBRR beyond the project's duration?

Institutionalization was rated on the third visit only, and the QACCs reported that a majority of the institutions (86 percent) embraced SBRR. Resource centers had been developed and were serving faculty, students, public school faculty, and parents. New faculty members were hired, and new textbooks and course materials were adopted. Literacy concentrations were available to graduates in elementary and middle school education. Partnerships with collaborating public schools were strengthened, and new partnerships showed promise for sustained relationships in the future. Assessment systems were updated and changed to reflect SBRR as a competency for graduates, and a strong indicator was seen when SBRR was specifically referenced in one school's conceptual framework. Only three institutions were rated unacceptable because their commitment to support SBRR was not evident.

Lessons Learned and Recommendations

The QACC site visit reports suggest that the RFTEN project made a strong impact on teacher candidates and PK–6 students. The engagement of RFTEN presidents and other senior-level administrators in the RFTEN project, coupled with QACC support, played a key role in successful implementation of the RFTEN model and SBRR on the campuses. QACCs successfully monitored, recorded, and supported institutional progress in implementing the RFTEN model. As coaches, QACCs were seen as nonthreatening and provided support, encouragement, and direction to institutions as needed.

QACCs were integral to the work of the RFTEN project and its ability to achieve its goals and mission. By the third site visit, SBRR was evident in the reading and the elementary instructional curriculum in most of the institutions; faculty members, students, and, in some instances, parents were using the resources; candidates were practicing SBRR with children in real classrooms in a variety of traditional and nontraditional settings; the degree of change had increased; and there was strong evidence of institutionalization.

The evaluation and analysis of QACC site visit reports also led to the following conclusions:

- Strong administrative and institutional support is needed for effective change in programs and curricula. It was the opinion of many QACCS that if institutional support was not present beyond the funding, then in many instances the RFTEN project probably would not continue.
- A well-trained reading faculty is needed for successful implementation of SBRR and the teacher preparation program. Faculty have to be supported if they are going to continue to improve and enhance the way candidates are prepared to teach reading using evidence-based reading instruction. To that end, faculty need opportunities for ongoing and focused professional development. That does not always entail financial support to attend conferences, although that is certainly viable. What faculty members need are time and opportunities to network and dialogue with each other about what is going on in their respective programs.

- Programs should be aligned with maintaining NCATE, International Reading Association, National Association for the Education of Young Children, and Association for Childhood Education International standards. Accountability was present in all RFTEN institutions to maintain and prepare teachers to meet local, state, and national standards.

- Liberal arts and science faculty should be engaged in improving the reading skills of teacher candidates. One institution collaborated with its School of Liberal Arts and established a professional development unit to provide support (workshops, seminars, resources, etc.) for education and liberal arts faculty.

- In an era of accountability and budget constraints, it is important to have well-developed plans for program evaluation and to determine the impact candidates will have on classroom learning. This requires closer collaboration and trusting relationships with public school systems. The project spawned pilot studies and other research studies to document program effectiveness and P–6 student learning. As reading is a critical skill for our nation's children, more research documenting effective strategies is warranted.

An Analysis of Intended and Unintended Outcomes of RFTEN

JOHN TAYLOR

This chapter analyzes the meaning of intended and unintended outcomes of the RFTEN project to implement scientifically based reading research (SBRR) practices in selected minority-serving institutions. The analysis is based on an examination of site-visit reports prepared by external evaluators and internal evaluation documents produced by project staff over a three-year period. I served as one of fourteen external reviewers of these RFTEN site-visit reports, and from this vantage point I offer perspectives on project outcomes.

I look at project outcomes, related literature on SBRR, and teacher education to inform discussions about the effectiveness and meaning of RFTEN (2003) in the larger education arena. In addition, I use evaluation theories and practices to examine certain outcomes that establish RFTEN as a landmark implementation grant project. I approached this analysis by asking what impact did RFTEN and the focus on SBRR have on the project's minority-serving partner institutions?

Key among the RFTEN evaluation documents is the report by Littleton and White (2006), *Analyzing RFTEN Site Visit Reports Inclusivity and Exemplary Reading Instruction: SBRR and the Preservice Preparation of Minority Teachers*. My discussion of the significance of the RFTEN project also reflects and is guided by professional judgment and educational experiences.

Background

The No Child Left Behind Act of 2001 (2002) established the Reading First program for all students in the nation. Substantive elements of Reading First build on the findings about SBRR documented by the National Reading Panel (2000). Reading First is a focused nationwide effort to enable all students to become confident and accomplished early readers. The U.S. Department of Education (2006) allocated funds to assist states and local school districts in eliminating reading deficiencies by developing high-quality, comprehensive SBRR instruction in grades K–3. The Reading First program design supports implementation and professional development opportunities for teachers in the use of SBBR. It also ensures school accountability through ongoing, valid, and reliable screening, diagnostic, and classroom-based assessment (http://www.ed.gov/programs/readingfirst/index.html).

The National Reading Panel (NRP) subgroups produced numerous reports in six chapters (National Institute of Child Health and Human Development, 2000a) and provided recommendations for reading instruction and evidence-based strategies for incorporating reading research into professional development and preservice education programs. It is clear that RFTEN embraced findings from the NRP, focusing its attention on the following NRP reports found in Chapter 4, Part II, "Teacher Preparation and Comprehension Strategies for Instruction," and in Chapter 5, "Teacher Education and Reading Instruction." Chapter 4 advanced the statements "Teachers can be taught to teach comprehension strategies effectively" and "Teaching comprehension strategies effectively in the natural setting of the classroom involves a level of proficiency and flexibility that often requires substantial and intensive teacher preparation" (p. 4–126). These conclusions are related to the emphasis in Chapter 5 of the NRP report on the importance of "extended training with ongoing support" in the preparation of teachers for reading instruction (p. 5–2). Both chapters reveal that appropriate teacher education and professional development produce higher achievement in students.

RFTEN's Impact on Partner Colleges and Universities

I approached the analysis of the project's intended and unintended outcomes by asking how it affected the implementation of SBRR strategies at partner colleges and universities. My analysis was guided by the theory of action, impact theory, and impact assessment principles.

The theory of action (King, Morris, & Fitz-Gibbon, 1987) links a project's goals and its intended and unintended outcomes. The theory relates project activities to short-term outcomes for faculty members, preservice teachers, school personnel, and

K–12 students (e.g., mentoring and tutoring) and *long-term* outcomes for institutions, teacher education programs (e.g., new curricula), and K–12 students (e.g., test score results). I determined that RFTEN exceeded the stakeholders' short- and long-term expectations for project outcomes.

Unintended outcomes may emerge when participants confront inescapable controversial issues such as the reputation of teacher education in the nation, perceptions about economically disadvantaged children, and the ability of minority students to learn. I view unintended outcomes as those that demonstrate how the RFTEN project successfully navigated challenges to exceed expectations.

Impact theory (Rossi, Lipsey, & Freeman, 2004) is causal. I used it to make assumptions about the project's primary processes, influences, and outcomes. The assumption is that exposure to and implementation of SBRR practices impacted institutions of higher education and improved teacher education programs. I established early on that all RFTEN primary goals and objectives were measured and met to some degree.

In examining RFTEN's influence, I used impact assessment to gauge how successfully the project implemented SBRR practices in institutions of higher education. Specifically, impact assessment helped to determine whether the desired outcomes were attained and whether those outcomes included changes, unintended side effects or consequences, or chain-reaction problems. In the words of Rossi, Lipsey, and Freeman (2004), "impact assessment involves producing an estimate of the *net effect* of a program—changes brought about by the intervention above and beyond those resulting from other processes and events affecting the targeted social condition" (p. 140).

RFTEN's Intended and Unintended Outcomes

One intended outcome was the project's impact on university presidents and deans and their response to RFTEN's top-down approach. This outcome also encompasses college/school partnerships—a hallmark of the project—which created an opportunity for faculty and teacher candidates to collaborate with classroom teachers and children in local low-performing, hard-to-staff, and Reading First schools.

It appears that the project functioned as intended. The structure of the project, staff, resources, and organization remained in place throughout its duration. Equally important, it is evident that the RFTEN team at the partner institutions (faculty, deans, and presidents) worked diligently to embrace, implement, and institutionalize the project's mission and goals. However, RFTEN internal and external evaluation reports, newsletters, and other publications and documents from 2006 show that at times the stability of the project's operations and infrastructure were challenged by administrative and leadership changes and faculty attrition.

Another intended outcome I observed is the positioning of minority-serving institutions as models. Other institutions nationwide can learn from the infusion of SBRR into teacher education programs and construct similar programs. The RFTEN project ushered in a new paradigm in teacher preparation. It realized a university and school partnership model that Zimpher and Howey (2005) strongly recommended for aligning the redesign of a teacher education program with a school reform initiative.

A further intended outcome was the manner in which RFTEN fostered collaboration. The higher education institution/school partnerships allowed teacher candidates to gain field experience, support from classroom teachers, and practical knowledge in tutoring and mentoring young readers enrolled in low-performing, hard-to-staff, and Reading First schools. RFTEN project participants were interested and committed professionals who often saw a connection between their institution's mission and that of the RFTEN project.

A second important collaboration was seen as RFTEN cultivated and nurtured the capacity of institutions and faculty to conduct research into teacher education by providing opportunities for university colleagues with research expertise to partner and network on research projects and to access funding.

RFTEN instituted a presidential top-down policy implementation approach to support project implementation at its partner institutions. The approach had both intended and unintended outcomes. The minority-serving institutions operated independently of each other, and thus RFTEN provides lessons for future policy study of top-down mandates at heterogeneous institutions (Heck, 2004). RFTEN demonstrated an understanding of the contextual conditions—institutional politics, organizational arrangement, cultural norms and belief systems, and institutional governance—that influenced program activity, acceptance, and implementation. The minority-serving institutions in the project saw RFTEN and its leadership as trusted partners, which allowed them to achieve intended shared goals. This is significant in a project such as RFTEN that incorporated and relied on a presidential top-down leadership approach to engage and create buy-in among college deans, department heads, and faculty to support curriculum and program changes within colleges of teacher education (American Council on Education, 1999).

Certain unintended outcomes are evident from a review of RFTEN's impact on the creation of institutional models at the project's colleges and universities. These models help us understand the vagaries of institutional policies, identify campus obstacles to change, and address time factors in implementation of intervention projects such as RFTEN on campus and in schools.

It is clear that there were pressures on colleges and schools of education nationwide to step up the pace of instituting SBRR (National Institute of Child Health and Human Development, 2000b; Shavelson & Towne, 2002; U.S. Department of Education, 2003). In addition, studies and reports published by prominent researchers and endorsed by educational organizations produced strong pressure to encourage improvements, redesign, and change in teacher education programs (National Commission on Teaching and America's Future, 2003; National Research Council, 2004; Darling-Hammond, 2006; Cochran-Smith & Zeichner, 2005; National Council on Teacher Quality, 2006). One unintended outcome for RFTEN participants was the means to respond directly to national pressures to implement scientific research by introducing SBRR to faculty in targeted teacher education reading programs.

Another unintended outcome is the way RFTEN successfully implemented SBRR and included evidence-based findings and recommendations from such education organizations as the American Educational Research Association Panel (Cochran-Smith & Zeichner, 2005; Schalock, Schalock, & Ayres, 2006), the National Academy of Education's Committee on Teacher Education (Darling-Hammond & Bransford, 2005), the National Center for Educational Statistics (Guarino, Hamilton, & Lockwood, 2006), and the Education Commission of the States (2006; Sanders, 2004). This effort was never stated as an outcome. Why? Because RFTEN's NCATE-accredited institutions meet accreditation standards designed to accommodate research (Wise, 2005).

Current tensions and criticisms faced by teacher education programs are reflected in an ongoing National Research Council study of teacher education (2004) and in the National Council on Teacher Quality's report *What Education Schools Aren't Teaching about Reading and What Elementary Teachers Aren't Learning* (NCTQ, 2006). The NRC study is in its third year. The NCTQ report found that of seventy-two education schools, only 15 percent provided future teachers with even minimal exposure to SBRR (p. 3). These findings were based on examinations of reading courses, syllabi, reading texts, and how well courses integrated SBRR practices. The RFTEN project and its partner institutions are demonstrating to the nation how to redesign and transform teacher preparation using evidence-based reading research. RFTEN demonstrates why the federal government and the higher education community must continue to recognize and support the implementation of SBRR for reaching young and struggling readers and ultimately closing the achievement gap in reading.

The RFTEN project was designed to provide training in evidence-based reading instruction at selected minority-serving institutions—an intended outcome. The result has been creative and effective teaching models that incorporate SBRR and the five components of essential reading to enhance and support reading achievement among struggling, disadvantaged, and minority readers.

RFTEN's top-down approach prompted positive impact from college presidents and deans who promoted and supported the project on their campuses. Top-down decision making by university administrators, regardless of the reason, was risky because of shared governance agreements in the academic climate in which they exist. Shared governance and policy pertains to roles faculty, administrators, and governing bodies play in the decision-making process on key programs, curricular and other changes, improvements, and reforms. The spirit of the policy is consultation, but requires presidents and other administrators to use discretion to make decisions implicating personnel (Lechuga, 2004). Administrators who accepted or at times used this leadership approach handled shared governance with tremendous finesse. They also maintained positive attitudes and respect toward university personnel and school communities in carrying out the RFTEN project.

It appears that even when a few teacher education programs make remarkable contributions (Dean, Lauer, & Urquhart (2005), it does not lessen the overall criticism of teacher education in higher education institutions (Huang & Haycock, 2002). The foregoing analysis is presented to bring into focus the value of the RFTEN project and its importance in changing attitudes about teacher education programs' contributions to society. There are 1,500 education programs across the nation, and RFTEN appears to have had a positive influence on 25 of them. Even when they were faced with the internal and external challenges in teacher education, RFTEN presidents and deans were able to respond effectively, support department heads and faculty, and demonstrate positive movement in their teacher education programs, even when faced with and responding to top-down mandates. In my opinion, this is an unintended outcome

Summary

The leadership of the RFTEN project did a superb job of proving the rationale for bridging two distinct educational and social milieus around SBRR practices In fact, the project related the mission of its minority-serving institutions to the imperative for action to address the reading deficiencies of economically challenged children in low-performing and hard-to-staff schools. This was accomplished by strategically linking the improvement of students' ability to read and the preparation of highly qualified teachers for those students. The implementation of SBRR at minority-serving institutions and public schools was well accepted. If there were barriers, they were likely related to the process of program implementation—how the universities and schools arranged time and schedules for mentoring, tutoring, and student teaching assignments in situ—not the purpose or goal of implementation.

The intended impact on RFTEN's university/school partnerships was realized, in the words of Darling-Hammond (2006), when the process matched their goals and both parties agreed to transform "the kinds of settings in which novices learn to teach and later become teachers . . . [and] ventured out further and further from the university and engage[d] ever more closely with schools in a mutual transformation agenda, with all of the struggle and messiness that implies" (p. 302). Throughout the RFTEN project, administrators and faculty likely learned that maintaining partnerships that transform teacher education requires attention to the conditions for nurturing, expanding, and strengthening such partnerships. Such meaningful partnerships need to be expanded. According to Zimpher and Howey (2005), university and school partnerships can be more meaningful if more bold redesigns happen in school reform initiatives. Zimpher and Howey contend that "[i]n spite of inhibiting conditions that exist in K–12 education, there exist nationally very few, if any, systematic efforts that truly align the redesign of teacher education with school reform. This is because there are few partnerships or inter-institutional arrangements between K–12 school sector and universities located in those communities bold enough to ensure that teacher preparation addresses directly the needs of schools and schools address classroom and school organization" (p. 266).

The minority-serving institutions participating in RFTEN should not be perceived as monolithic. Although they were part of a unique consortium of teacher education colleges, RFTEN institutions operated independently, often adapting the project model and SBRR strategies to respond to the specific needs of their teacher candidates, faculty, administration, community, and constituents. To that extent, differences in project outcomes were expected. This fact is pertinent, especially when we know that RFTEN presidents and deans participated in the same briefings and trainings. Those administrators still had to adapt what they learned into language and messages that fit the realities of their institutional contexts. This was also true for RFTEN-trained faculty responsible for preparing teacher candidates (Weiss, 1972).

Impact assessment asks whether the desired outcomes were attained and whether those changes had unintended side effects or consequences (Rossi, Lipsey, & Freeman, 2004). Certainly, these consequences were attended to as necessary with diplomacy and respect. In some ways, the RFTEN evaluation design (Elliott, 2006) accounted for those participating in the project achieving similar goals yet having different outcomes. As "reflective practitioners," some RFTEN institutions followed different and creative paths (processes) to meet the project's objectives and goals.

Providing teacher educators and ultimately classroom teachers with professional development opportunities and access to the best available SBRR served to make RFTEN a success. In addition, RFTEN effectively managed a high-quality initiative that influenced and engaged presidents and deans and used evidence to transform how teacher candidates learn to teach reading and ultimately how children in the classroom learn to read. RFTEN offers valuable lessons and has provided minority-serving institutions with the resources and platform to transform teacher education and reading achievement.

References

American Council on Education. (1999). *To touch the future: Transforming the way teachers are taught.* Washington, DC: American Council on Education.

Cochran-Smith, M. & K. M. Zeichner. (Eds.). (2005). *Studying teacher education: The report of the AERA panel on research and teacher education.* Mahwah, NJ: Lawrence Erlbaum.

Darling-Hammond, L. (2006). Constructing 21st-century teacher education. *Journal of Teacher Education, 57* (3), 300–314.

Darling-Hammond, L. & J. Bransford. (Eds.). (2005). *Preparing teachers for a changing world.* San Francisco: Jossey-Bass.

Dean, C., P. Lauer, & V. Urquhart. (2005). Outstanding teacher education programs: What do they have that the others don't? *Phi Delta Kappan, 87* (4), 284–289

Education Commission of the States. (2006). Reference: Reading First state plans. Retrieved April 26, 2006, from http://www.ecs.org.

Elliott, E. (2006). A look at evaluation in RFTEN's culminating year. *First Read, 2* (3), 4–5.

Guarino, C. M., L. S. Hamilton, & J. R. Lockwood. (2006). *Teacher qualifications, instructional practices, and reading and mathematics gains of kindergartners.* U.S. Department of Education Institute of Education Sciences (NCES) 2006–031 Research and Development Report.

Heck, R. H. (2004). *Studying educational and social policy: Theoretical concepts and research methods.* Mahwah, NJ: Lawrence Erlbaum.

Huang, S., Y. Yi, & K. Haycock. (2002). *Interpret with caution: The first state Title II reports on the quality of teacher preparation.* Washington, DC: The Education Trust.

King, J. A., L. L. Morris, & C. T. Fitz-Gibbon. (1987). *How to assess program implementation.* Thousand Oaks, CA: Sage.

Lechuga, V.M. (2004). Exploring current issues on shared governance. *New Directions for Higher Education, 127,* 95–98.

Littleton, D.M., & White, M.C. (2006). *Analyzing RFTEN Site Visit Reports: Inclusivity and Exemplary Reading Instruction: SBRR and the Preservice Preparation of Minority Teachers.* Unpublished report, Washington, DC: RFTEN

National Commission on Teaching and America's Future. (2003). *No dream denied: A pledge to America's children.* Washington, DC: The National Commission on Teaching and America's Future.

National Council on Teacher Quality. (2006). *What education schools aren't teaching about reading and what elementary teachers aren't learning.* Retrieved June 23, 2006 from, http://www.nctq.org.

National Institute of Child Health and Human Development. (2000a). *Report of the National Reading Panel, teaching children to read: An evidence-based assessment of the scientific research literature on reading instruction. Reports of the Subgroups* (NIH Publication No. 00–4754). Washington, DC: U.S. Government Printing Office. (NIH Publication no. 00–4769)

National Institute of Child Health and Human Development. (2000b). *Report of the National Reading Panel, teaching children to read: An evidence-based assessment of the scientific research literature on reading instruction.* (NIH Publication no. 00–4769) Washington, DC: U.S. Government Printing Office

National Research Council. (2004). *National Research Council Teacher Preparation Study: Teacher Preparation Programs in the United States.* Washington, DC: National Academies of Sciences, Division on Behavioral and Social Sciences and Education.

No Child Left Behind Act of 2001, (2002) PUB. L. No. 107–110,115 Stat. 1425.

RFTEN (2003). Reading First Teacher Preparation Reading Excellence Network Initiative: Preparing highly qualified teachers to leave no child behind. A proposal submitted to the U.S. Department of Education, September 3, 2003.

Rossi, P. H., M. W. Lipsey, & H. E. Freeman. (2004). *Evaluation: A systematic approach* (7th ed.). Thousand Oaks, CA: Sage.

Sanders, T. (2004). No time to waste: The vital role of college and university leaders in improving science and mathematics education. Paper presented at the Invitational Conference on Teacher Preparation and Institutions of Higher Education: Mathematics and Science Content Knowledge. U.S. Department of Education.

Schalock, H. D., M. D. Schalock, & R. Ayres. (2006). Scaling up research in teacher education: New demands on theory, measurement, and design. *Journal of Teacher Education*, 57 (2), 102–119.

Shavelson, R. J. & L. Towne. (Eds.). (2002). *Scientific research in education.* Washington, DC: National Academy Press.

U.S. States Department of Education (2003). *Identifying and Implementing Educational Practices Supported by Rigorous Evidence: A User Friendly Guide.* Washington, DC: Coalition for Evidence-Based Policy. Retrieved December 8, 2003 at http://www.excelgov.org/evidence; Also available at http://www.ed.gov/rschstat/research/pubs/rigorousevid/guide_pg3.html.

U.S. Department of Education. (2006). Reading First awards. Retrieved April 26, 2006, from http://www.ed.gov/programs/readinfirst/awards.html.

Weiss, C. H. (1972). *Evaluation research: Methods for assessing program effectiveness.* Upper Saddle River, NJ: Prentice-Hall.

Wise, A. E. (2005). Establishing teaching as a profession: The essential role of professional accreditation. *Journal of Teacher Education*, 56 (4), 318–331.

Zimpher, N. L., & Howey, K.R. (2005). The politics of partnerships for teacher education design and school renewal. *Journal of Teacher Education*, 56 (3), 266–271.

RFTEN

Implications for Addressing the Achievement Gap in Reading and in Mathematics

LECRETIA A. BUCKLEY

Inequities continue to be part of the educational experience of many of our nation's students. In particular, students of color and students from low socioeconomic backgrounds often lack access to quality teaching, resources, and adequate facilities in which to learn and thrive. Since the commemoration of the fiftieth anniversary of the *Brown v. Board of Education* decision and the 2001 passage of the No Child Left Behind Act (NCLB), the courts and legislation have been employed to improve educational opportunities. Scholars continue to review the decision, examining its impact and its possible unanticipated outcomes (e.g., Tate, Ladson-Billings, & Grant; 1993; Ladson-Billings, 2004).

In 2003, RFTEN became the only higher education initiative funded through the NCLB. In just three years, RFTEN provided a promising picture of what is possible and what is needed to address the nation's widening achievement gap in reading and to create strategies for equitable education. This chapter examines RFTEN project implementation and its implications for responding to the achievement gap in mathematics education. The goals of the RFTEN project, as I see them, were driven by the widening achievement gap in reading and the need to empower education faculty at minority-serving institutions. But RFTEN's ultimate aim was to make a difference in America's classrooms to support struggling readers and to empower classroom teachers to teach reading effectively using scientifically based reading research (SBRR) strategies.

Addressing Critical Factors in Student Achievement

The nation's achievement gaps in reading and in mathematics are troubling and persistent phenomena. The National Assessment of Educational Progress (NAEP) data reveal that students of color and poor students attain significantly lower achievement levels than their white, middle-class counterparts (Lubienski, 2002; National Center for Education Statistics [NCES], 2005a,b). Even when students of color make academic gains, they tend to be on low-level skills (Tate, 1997) or not to be statistically significant (NCES, 2005a,b). Reading and mathematics results summarized in *The Nation's Report Card* (2005a, 2005b) illustrate that although white, black, and Hispanic students are experiencing small gains in academic achievement, a persistent and significant gap remains. In reading at grade 4, the achievement gap between white and black students and between white and Hispanic students narrowed in the past two decades; however, the change was not statistically significant. In mathematics at grade 8, the gains experienced between 1990 and 2005 remained insignificant. Further analysis of NAEP data on mathematics achievement revealed that students of color and poor students have fewer opportunities to experience instructional practices advocated by leading professional organizations or identified as best practices in their subject matter areas (Lubienski & Crockett, 2007). The NCLB and these analyses of national data have intensified awareness of the need to improve academic achievement for *all* students. If progress in narrowing the achievement gap is to be made, then efforts must focus on empowering large numbers of teachers and teacher educators, as RFTEN maintains.

Although the crucial role of teachers in narrowing the achievement gap and providing a high-quality education to students is undeniable, they face many obstacles. Teacher candidates need to prepare for teaching in classrooms that are racially and ethnically diverse (Cockrell, Placier, Cockrell, & Middleton, 1999; Sleeter, 2001). Students graduating from the nation's teachers colleges are disproportionately white, female, lower- or middle-class, and often are provincial people who feel unprepared to teach racial and ethnic minority children (Wideen, Mayer-Smith, & Moon, 1998; Terrill & Mark, 2000; Dee & Henkin, 2002). The lack of highly qualified teachers presents a challenge to which the RFTEN project responded in its focus on teacher preparation in reading while building institutional capacity for sustainability.

In addition to equipping teachers with SBRR strategies and training, RFTEN sought to focus on teacher candidates being trained at selected minority-serving institutions. RFTEN's rationale was that a large number of minority teachers in public schools earn their undergraduate degrees at minority-serving institutions, and a significant proportion of these teachers teach minority students in hard-to-staff and low-performing schools. Therefore, preparing preservice teachers to use SBRR would be an important step in impacting the reading achievement of P–12 students (RFTEN, 2006, pp. 6–7).

Thus, RFTEN's focus on teacher candidates at these institutions addressed an overarching concern in the field regarding racial and ethnic diversity among teachers. It also addressed concerns about teachers not understanding the specific needs of poor and minority children and feeling ill prepared to teach these students.

Professional Development and Sustainability: Preparing New Teachers

Using professional development, training, and resources aimed at engaging teacher educators and administrators, the RFTEN project was able to create promising models of sustainability among its partner institutions. The sustainability of efforts is a prerequisite if the national achievement gap in reading is to be narrowed. Opportunities to build the capacity of RFTEN partner institutions to further the project's goals beyond the life of the three-year grant came largely from the professional development activities. In particular, RFTEN incorporated several principles that are hallmarks of a consensus model for highly effective professional development (Hawley & Valli, 1999). These principles resulted from an analysis of site visit reports and ongoing assessments of RFTEN partner institutions. I was part of a fourteen-member team of scholars and external evaluators selected to review these findings and documents. These principles and the professional development activities address the development of teacher education candidates as well as teacher educators.

The first principle of the RFTEN project was a focus on student learning. SBRR addresses what is known about a child's ability to learn to read. The support mechanisms, resources, course revision, development, and field or clinical experiences in local schools focused on increasing awareness and understanding of SBRR. The particular efforts of the institutions were also aimed at providing opportunities for teacher candidates to learn, practice, and implement evidence-based reading strategies.

The RFTEN project model was campus based, a second principle of highly effective professional development. Quality assurance coaching consultants (QACCs) visited RFTEN partner institutions and assisted administrators and faculty in developing plans for integrating SBRR strategies into teacher education programs. These once-per-semester QACC visits supported the work of RFTEN faculty teams and the development and implementation of the RFTEN SBRR models. These RFTEN technical consultants also helped faculty and administrators devise plans for building on the resources and infrastructure already in place at their institutions and helped them to identify resources or develop new frameworks.

Third, RFTEN's implementation was collaborative. The project encouraged, enhanced, and fostered collaboration and information sharing among RFTEN and other faculty at its partner institutions. Some RFTEN faculty successfully engaged their colleagues outside of education, sharing their RFTEN training and resources and SBRR strategies.

External participants included the QACCs, consultants, members of the P–6 school systems, and parents. These participants provided multiple perspectives and varied expertise that aided in the identification of program or institutional weaknesses and the development of plans to address them. Such buy-in by an array of stakeholders further suggests increased sustainability of the project and SBRR instruction.

Fourth, the RFTEN project took the perspective of teacher educators into account as plans were developed. This principle is referred to as being *teacher directed*. Teacher educators revised their syllabi as a result of those plans. Because institutions used their assessment system to inform education program evaluation, teacher educators participated in programmatic revisions.

A fifth feature, subject matter specificity characterizes the RFTEN project. There is compelling evidence that professional development that focuses on subject matter is more effective than experiences that do not. In an atmosphere that sometimes emphasizes general approaches to improving achievement, such as test-taking strategies, the RFTEN project and participants at each of the institutions focused their efforts on reading, and in particular on teaching reading effectively using SBRR.

These five features—(1) a focus on student learning, (2) school-based implementation, (3) collaboration, (4) a teacher-directed approach, and (5) a focus on subject matter—have significantly impacted the implementation of RFTEN's methods by the majority of participating institutions. However, this analysis has not addressed two other principles that have been identified as distinguishing features of the consensus model of highly effective professional development.

Those two principles are inquiry orientation and continuity. First, data and the evaluation reports on the RFTEN grant were not designed to sufficiently address the inquiry-oriented principle. An inquiry-oriented approach entails collaborative problem solving whereby teachers call their own practices into question. Second, it is inappropriate to evaluate how enduring the practices and changes that resulted from the RFTEN project will be since the project operated only for three years, the life of the grant. The tenure of some institutional cohorts in the project was less than three years. It appears, however, that several measures are in place to support the sustainability of the RFTEN model and strategies.

Sustainability: Institutional Capacity and Teacher Education Programs

Two notions—sustainability and implications beyond reading—can be used to explain what RFTEN can offer to the larger educational community. The positive outcomes that RFTEN has achieved must be sustainable to have a lasting national impact on the achievement gap. Here, I outline the degree to which the RFTEN project was likely to promote sustainability. The outline includes highlights from analyses of site visit reports and addresses institutional support and the sustainability of SBRR strategies in teacher education programs.

Institutional support was strong among the thirty-one participating institutions in Cohorts 1 and 2, with 84 percent of the reports from site visits assigning a rating of at least acceptable.[1] Institutional support included the active participation of university presidents, deans, and other administrators. Active support from administration took the form of participation in RFTEN meetings, nomination of RFTEN efforts for awards, and additional funding. Institutional support was enhanced by two other features that promoted institutionalization—signs of institutional change and institutional capacity. Signs that institutional change was already underway were identified approximately 80 percent of the time. These signs included course revisions, the addition of new reading courses, strategic hires, and field and clinical experiences that provided teacher candidates with opportunities to implement SBRR practices. Institutional capacity, or a commitment to support SBRR after the project, was extensive.

An acceptable rating was assigned 84 percent of the time, This capacity was demonstrated differently across institutions and included (1) the creation of reading centers that facilitated collaboration among colleges, universities, and P–6 schools; (2) the offering of literacy concentrations; and (3) the revision of teacher education program assessment systems and conceptual frameworks to reflect SBRR. Institutions also took advantage of available resources, and the utilization of these resources increased over the course of the project. Following the second site visit, 75 percent of the institutions received at least an acceptable rating, and 89 percent received at least an acceptable rating during the third visit.

Although the importance of institutional support is undeniable, the practices of teacher education programs must exemplify the conceptual underpinnings espoused in SBRR. In other words, one ought to be able to look at the everyday practices within the teacher education programs and see signs of the changes that have been reported. In RFTEN, those signs were promising. In particular, the teacher education programs were engaging in efforts designed to support the sustainability of practices implemented as a result of the project. These changes were both associated with individual courses and programmatic. Preexisting courses were revised, and field and clinical experiences were enhanced or transformed to reflect SBRR and to include opportunities for teacher candidates to practice and implement SBRR strategies. Strategic hires were made to ensure faculty expertise in reading and literacy. These and other changes led the external evaluation team to score the institutions as being at or above the acceptable range 74 percent of the time. A key indicator of programmatic change was an integrated assessment system. Eighty-six percent of the institutions received a rating of at least acceptable for having such an assessment system that could be used to evaluate the program. Institutions also used licensure data for program evaluations, and 82 percent of the ratings were acceptable or above on this measure.

Implications beyond Reading

In a short time, RFTEN demonstrated that a highly effective professional development project can be implemented with significant positive outcomes in multiple settings. Indeed, more in-depth evaluations and research are warranted to add to our understanding of what works in implementing such a far-reaching program. The RFTEN project has embarked on a major undertaking, and the successes that have been demonstrated offer us insights for literacy and beyond. I claim that those who engage in, design, and study professional development can also garner insights. I also believe the field of mathematics education can benefit from these insights since the achievement gap in mathematics is similarly long standing. There are parallels between reading and mathematics to support my claim that mathematics education can benefit from the lessons learned through the implementation of RFTEN.

In the *Reading Framework for the 2005 National Assessment of Educational Progress* (National Assessment Governing Board, 2004), reading includes "the ability to understand and use written texts for enjoyment and to learn, to participate in society, and to achieve one's goals" (p. 7). The National Council of Teachers of Mathematics (NCTM, 2000) identifies a similar need for mathematics, asserting that "the need to understand and be able to use mathematics in everyday life and in the workplace has never been greater and will continue to increase" (p. 4). Like reading, mathematics involves sense making and doing. Reading and math skills are essential as we live, work, and participate in society indeed, they operate as gatekeepers to economic and democratic participation.

In this vein, the NCTM (2000) further argued that "a society in which only a few have the mathematical knowledge needed to fill crucial economic, political, and scientific roles is not consistent with the values of a just democratic system or its economic needs" (p. 5). Mathematics has been employed, historically, as a filter limiting or defining, a priori, students' opportunities. Volmink (1994, p. 51) argued that mathematics has been used as a "judge, in order to decide who in society 'can' and who 'cannot.'" The critical role of reading and mathematics adds to the urgency to address the inequities that plague these areas of education. The achievement gap in each of these fields encapsulates these inequities and sets the stage for discussing parallels and the accompanying obstacles that must be overcome. Because of the numerous parallels, insights from approaches to reading may be productive in addressing the achievement gap in mathematics. In the following pages, I discuss other parallels—developing a research base and changing views on who *can* learn. These offer hope of continued improvements.

The recognition of the critical role that reading and mathematics play in opening or closing doors to educational and economic opportunities has been coupled with changes in perspective about who can learn to read and who can do mathematics. It has been a long-standing view that not all students can learn mathematics. In fact, analyses of data from international studies suggest that this view is more common in the United States than in other countries. But progress is being made.

Changes in the field can be traced to *Everybody Counts: A Report to the Nation on the Future of Mathematics Education* (National Research Council, 1989). This document ties opportunities to mathematical knowledge and asserts that *all* students can learn mathematics. This view was shared by the NCTM (1989) in its first standards document, *Curriculum and Evaluation Standards for School Mathematics*, and receives increased attention in the latest standards document, *Principles and Standards for School Mathematics* (*PSSM*) (NCTM, 2000). In *PSSM*, the equity principle, the first of six principles[2] for ensuring a high-quality mathematics education for all students, states that "excellence in mathematics education requires equity—high expectations and strong support for all students" (p. 11).

Research has been conducted into views about who can learn mathematics and how varied expectations impact curriculum and instruction (Wiley & Eskilson, 1978; Beady & Hansell, 1981; Irvine & York, 1993; Stodolsky & Grossman, 2000). This research is closely linked to tracking practices that continue disproportionately and negatively to impact students of color and poor students in the United States (Oakes, 1990; Oakes, Wells, Jones, & Datnow, 1996). These views are deeply embedded and are linked to biological explanations of intelligence and views of ability as fixed and innate (Oakes Wells, Jones, & Datnow, 1996). The NCTM espouses a view of equitable mathematics education that "challenges a pervasive societal belief in North America that only some students are capable of learning mathematics" (p. 12).

The field of mathematics education is making progress as systematic investigations examine pedagogical approaches that enhance student understanding and increase achievement (Grouws, 1992; Kilpatrick, Martin, & Schifter, 2003). This research base provides an analog to SBRR.

The research base on the teaching and learning of mathematics focused greater attention on the need to address the achievement gap in mathematics and the need to prepare teachers to teach racially and ethnically diverse students. The promising outcomes already demonstrated by the RFTEN project are informative to the mathematics education community and to the larger educational community. RFTEN's efforts and accomplishments will greatly inform how professional development can be beneficial and which aspects of RFTEN can be used to impact math achievement for P–6 students through professional development for teachers.

Specifically, the implementation of RFTEN illustrates that the consensus model for high-quality professional development is effective. As discussed above, the thirty-one participating institutions are designing sustainable professional development, and consideration of a similar approach in mathematics is warranted.

Notes

1. The three possible ratings were unacceptable, acceptable, and target. The ratings were defined using the following rubrics: (1) unacceptable—report fails to provide evidence for this category; (2) acceptable—report provides adequate evidence for this category; and (3) target-report provides substantive evidence for this category.
2. The other five principles are curriculum, teaching, learning, assessment, and technology.

References

Beady, C. H. & S. Hansell. (1981). Teacher race and expectations for student achievement. *American Educational Research Journal*, 18 (2), 191–206.

Cockrell, K. S., P. L. Placier, H. Cockrell, & J. N. Middleton. (1999). Coming to terms with "diversity" and "multiculturalism" in teacher education: Learning about our students, changing our practice. *Teaching and Teacher Education*, 15, 351–366.

Dee, J. R. & A. B. Henkin. (2002). Assessing dispositions toward cultural diversity among preservice teachers. *Urban Education*, 37, 22–40.

Grouws, D. A. (Ed.). (1992). *Handbook of research on mathematics teaching and learning*. Reston, VA: National Council of Teachers of Mathematics.

Hawley, W. & L. Valli. (1999). The essentials of effective professional development: A new consensus. In L. Darling-Hammond & G. Sykes (Eds.), *Teaching as the learning profession: Handbook of policy and practice* (pp. 127–150). San Francisco: Jossey-Bass.

Irvine, J. J. & D. E. York. (1993). Teacher perspectives: Why do African-American, Hispanic, and Vietnamese students fail? In S. W. Rothstein (Ed.), *Handbook on schooling in urban America* (pp. 161–173). Westport, CT: Greenwood.

Kilpatrick, J., W. G. Martin, & D. Schifter. (Eds.) (2003). *A research companion to principles and standards for school mathematics*. Reston, VA: National Council of Teachers of Mathematics.

Ladson-Billings, G. (2004). Landing on the wrong note: The price paid for *Brown*. *Educational Researcher*, 33 (7), 3–13.

Lubienski, S. T. (2002). A closer look at black-white mathematics achievement gaps: Intersections of race and SES in NAEP achievement and instructional practices data. *The Journal of Negro Education*, 71 (4), 269–287.

Lubienski, S. T. & M. D. Crockett (2007). NAEP findings regarding race/ethnicity: Mathematics achievement, student affect, and school/home experiences. In P. Kloosterman & F. K. Lester (Eds.), *Results from the ninth mathematics assessment of NAEP* (pp. 227–260). Reston, VA: NCTM.

National Assessment Governing Board. (2004). *Reading framework for the 2005 National Assessment of Educational Progress*. Washington, DC: U.S. Government Printing Office.

National Center for Education Statistics (NCES). (2005a). *The nation's report card: Mathematics 2005*. Jessup, MD: NAEP.

———. (2005b). *The nation's report card: Reading 2005*. Jessup, MD: NAEP.

National Council of Teachers of Mathematics. (1989). *Curriculum and evaluation standards for school mathematics*. Reston, VA: NCTM.

———. (2000). *Principles and standards for school mathematics*. Reston, VA: NCTM.

National Research Council. (1989). *Everybody counts: A report to the nation on the future of mathematics education*. Washington, DC: National Academy Press.

Oakes, J. (1990). *Multiplying inequalities: The effects of race, social class, and tracking on opportunities to learn mathematics and science*. Santa Monica, CA: RAND Corp.

Oakes, J., A. S. Wells, M. Jones, & A. Datnow. (1996). Detracking: The social construction of ability, cultural politics, and resistance to reform. *Teachers College Record*, 98 (3), 482–510.

Reading First Teacher Education Network. (2006). *Analyzing the RFTEN site visit reports. Inclusivity and exemplary reading instruction: SBRR and the preservice preparation of minority teachers*. Washington, DC: National Council for Accreditation of Teacher Education.

Sleeter, C. (2001). Preparing teachers for culturally diverse schools: Research on the overwhelming presence of whiteness. *Journal of Teacher Education*, 52, 94–106.

Stodolsky, S. S. & P. L. Grossman. (2000). Changing students, changing teaching. *Teachers College Record*, 102 (1), 125–172.

Tate, W. F. (1997). Race-ethnicity, SES, gender, and language proficiency trends in mathematics achievement: An update. *Journal for Research in Mathematics Education*, 28, 652–697.

Tate, W. F., G. Ladson-Billings, C. A. Grant. (1993). The *Brown* decision revisited: Mathematizing social problems. *Educational Policy*, 7 (3), 255–275.

Terrill, M. & D. L. H. Mark. (2000). Preservice teachers' expectations for schools with children of color and second-language learners. *Journal of Teacher Education*, 51, 149–155.

Volmink, J. (1994). Mathematics by all. In S. Lerman (Ed.), *Cultural perspectives on the mathematics classroom* (pp. 51–67). Dordrecht, the Netherlands: Kluwer.

Wideen, M., J. Mayer-Smith, & B. Moon. (1998). A critical analysis of the research on learning to teach: Making the case for an ecological perspective on inquiry. *Review of Educational Research*, 68, 130–178.

Wiley, M. G. & A. Eskilson. (1978). Why did you learn in school today? Teachers' perceptions of causality. *Sociology of Education*, 51, 261–269.

Florida International University

RFTEN Collaboration Helps Prepare Reading Teachers for Changing Times

B. DENISE HAWKINS AND JOYCE C. FINE

Florida International University (FIU), a public research university with an urban campus, lies in the heart of southwest Miami-Dade County, a culturally rich and racially and ethnically diverse community. The entire South Florida region serves as a laboratory and clinical setting for the delivery of FIU's programs, including those offered by the College of Education. Founded in 1972 as Miami's first public university, FIU is young by higher education standards. By 2002, FIU received the Carnegie Classification as an Urban Research Level 1 Institution of Higher Education.

FIU was among the first twenty-five institutions tapped to participate in the RFTEN national reading initiative in 2003. When FIU entered the project, its College of Education was large, well established, thriving, and adhering to the practice of professional collaboration. The College of Education was nationally accredited; it had an exemplary reading component in its teacher preparation program offering four courses in reading, and it was facilitated by an academic structure informed by current research and based on professional standards mandated by both the State of Florida and the International Reading Association (IRA). Many RFTEN faculty at the College of Education believed that there was room to make an already great education and reading program better. The RFTEN faculty knew that they had to stay current and network with others in the profession if they were to prepare the best teachers for changing times. Although FIU had been engaged on a regional and national level with reading educators, attending conferences, and promoting professional development, they did not have the same leverage that being a part of a national network such as RFTEN provided.

FIU's ability to prepare the best teachers for changing times and dynamics in education demanded a response to the No Child Left Behind Act of 2001. The National Reading Panel's report was pivotal. It concluded that teachers must have in-depth knowledge of the essential components of reading and identified approaches that worked with students. FIU's participation in the RFTEN project, faculty said, helped extend their reach and value. To stay abreast of current reading strategies and best practices, FIU recognizes the need to network constantly and share and exchange information nationally with other teacher educators and administrators. RFTEN has provided the opportunities and the tools for this. Like their fellow RFTEN institutions, FIU's College of Education has gained access to leading reading and education experts, cutting-edge resources, and training in evidence-based reading strategies. In addition, being a part of the RFTEN initiative has enhanced faculty credibility not only with teacher candidates but with administrators and other faculty in the College of Education, RFTEN faculty reported.

By attending regularly scheduled RFTEN collaborative development seminars or training sessions, for example, the RFTEN faculty team was able to return to the classroom armed with materials, other RFTEN faculty contacts, and lecture notes and PowerPoint presentations, often from the same authors and reading experts their students were studying and reading about.

FIU's teacher candidates are in high demand, making up more than 25 percent of new teachers hired by the Miami-Dade County public school system each year. Today, those graduating from reading courses taught by RFTEN-trained faculty and armed with evidence-based reading strategies practiced with real children in the classroom are among the region's top hires. Many graduates and candidates report being hired on the spot or aggressively recruited when they come with demonstrated skills in reading instruction, especially those that work best with the burgeoning population of culturally, racially, and ethnically diverse children in Miami's public schools. As first-year teachers, most FIU graduates enter classrooms and public schools where Spanish and Creole are among the more than one hundred languages spoken (for most children, English is often a new or second language) and where white children are the minority. As one of the largest producers of Hispanic teachers in the nation, the College of Education at FIU faces a tremendous responsibility in preparing teachers who themselves are often first-generation college students whose first language is not English, who can teach reading to struggling readers, and who understand that diversity extends beyond culture, language, and skin color.

Preparing Reading Teachers:
A Look at the Teacher Preparation Program

The Department of Curriculum and Instruction in FIU's College of Education has been recognized for excellence in reading teacher preparation by the IRA several times. The Elementary Education program at FIU was named one of eight "exemplary" reading teacher preparation programs by the IRA when they became part of the National Commission on Excellence in Elementary Teacher Preparation for Reading Instruction. The Masters of Science in Reading Education at the College of Education has also achieved national recognition following rigorous review by the IRA and by the National Council for Accreditation of Teacher Education (NCATE). RFTEN's goals and mission, including implementing standards-based reading instruction and assessment and the integration of scientifically based reading research (SBRR) and best practice into program planning, reflect those of FIU's College of Education.

Candidates for the early childhood undergraduate degree complete three required reading courses, elementary education majors complete four required reading courses, and candidates preparing to teach at the secondary level complete a required course on reading in content area reading. Candidates in the elementary education program complete requirements for ESOL (English for speakers of other languages) endorsement. The reading courses required of candidates in early childhood and elementary education are sequential and progressive:

- *Course One* (Language and Literacy Development): orientation and overview regarding the discipline of reading. The purpose of the course is to provide candidates with foundational knowledge of the nature of language and of literacy development. The course focuses on the early development of literacy that all children go through as they interact in a literate environment.
- *Course Two* (Methods of Teaching Primary Literacy): the course concentrates on various methods for teaching reading. The purpose of this course is to develop candidates' knowledge base regarding children's early acquisition of literacy, as well as the use of that knowledge during actual classroom literacy instruction in the primary grades. The knowledge, skills, and dispositions developed in this course reflect the professional standards specified by the IRA and the Florida Accomplished Practices requirements and include current research and best practices identified by literacy teacher educators.
- *Course Three* (Methods of Teaching and Assessment of Reading): assessment tools and Basic Reading Inventory are introduced. This course seeks

to develop candidates' understanding, skills, and the dispositions necessary for teaching literacy in the intermediate grades. Writing as part of literacy development is introduced.

- *Course Four* (Content and Methods of Teaching Literacy in Schools): capstone practicum allowing candidates to implement theory in practice. This course (with embedded practicum) is designed to provide candidates with experience of demonstrating the knowledge and skills needed to teach literacy effectively to diverse populations. Candidates' understanding of how theory translates to practical application is developed. Here, the emphasis is on candidates learning how to assess students' reading ability and design instruction based on students' needs. This course is delivered as a practicum and is conducted in an elementary school setting. The candidates receive feedback and coaching on important practical experiences in implementing the information, knowledge, dispositions, and skills learned in previous reading instruction required in the teacher preparation programs.

The Fourth Course's Practicum: Creating an RFTEN Model in the College of Education's Teacher Preparation Program

FIU's College of Education prides itself on offering candidates a "quality curriculum, personalized interaction with students and openness to diversity." But RFTEN faculty declared the development of a fourth practicum course in the curriculum their "RFTEN project model or signature"—the one aspect of the project that distinguishes the FIU program from those of RFTEN's other thirty-seven institutions.

Although the State of Florida responded to the urgent need for highly qualified teachers in 2003 by mandating that a fourth reading course be added to the elementary education preparation programs of all of its institutions, RFTEN faculty at FIU said the move provided them with the opportunity to develop "what teacher education research indicated was needed." The additional course was Methods of Teaching Literacy in the Context of Schools. RFTEN had a significant effect on how that course was developed and implemented. This fourth course's practicum includes a supervised clinical experience component focused on the five essential elements of reading identified by the National Reading Panel—phonics, phonemic awareness, fluency, vocabulary, and comprehension—and on SBRR strategies supported by the RFTEN project.

What emerged in the College of Education was a fresh approach to teaching reading that provided intensive field experience, said RFTEN faculty who sought a departure from what they called "typical university preparation programs that teach reading based on a series of literacy courses coupled with limited field experience connected to coursework." There is no substitute for candidates gaining firsthand experience in the field, they said, referring to some reading experts who employ technology to simulate or replace firsthand experience. Still other teacher educators in reading "have included one-on-one tutoring, but the process lacked direct supervision by a reading expert or faculty member," FIU's RFTEN faculty found. In FIU's model of reading teacher preparation, one-on-one clinical experience is a centerpiece that supports preservice teachers, the work of classroom teachers, and students. That clinical experience is supervised by reading experts who are faculty and graduate students. One of FIU's lecturers is a doctoral candidate with more than 30 years of classroom teaching experience. She and others intervene before student teaching to support candidates in learning the complexities of assessment and of giving instruction to low-performing, diverse students using SBRR.

In the College of Education at FIU, teaching reading in the context of schools both fits the conceptual framework and addresses the needs of preservice teachers. The components of this conceptual framework look like this:

- *Interconnectedness*: university course held on site; community partnership with the office of the mayor
- *Interculturalism*: addresses needs of a low-performing urban school for high-quality tutoring
- *Instructional leadership*: professional development for teachers at the school site
- *Inquiry*: allows research into the effects of the model of reading teacher preparation and retention

In the practicum course, preservice teachers provide ten weeks of tutoring and teaching for one hour, twice a week:

- Preservice teachers are supervised by faculty, who read and evaluate their lesson plans before the individual tutoring sessions. Those lesson plans are informed by assessments and tailored to meet the specific needs of their assigned students.
- Preservice teachers provide high-quality one-on-one tutoring.
- Students build disposition to work with diverse populations.
- Since most newly hired teachers are placed in inner-city schools, a supervised practicum helps to prepare them to meet the needs of all students.

The practicum experience provides the assessment and instruction cycle of the course. During the practicum, candidates are involved in tutoring elementary students at partner schools. Collaborations between an RFTEN institution and a local Reading First, hard-to-staff, or low-performing elementary school are hall-marks of the RFTEN project (and a requirement). The delivery of the practicum experience at FIU requires teacher candidates, before they participate in tutoring sessions, to create lesson plans that are evaluated by a professor. But RFTEN faculty admit that not all candidates are ready for the fourth course or clinical experience. Sometimes faculty must make the tough decision to have candidates repeat the class an additional semester. "It takes courage to say that we know what you need to do to teach reading well and therefore you have to wait [to do your student teaching]," said one RFTEN faculty member.

Professional Collaboration and Teacher Preparation

When teacher candidates begin the clinical portion of the practicum, they come with little experience in teaching reading—only what they have learned in the classroom, in field placements, or by reading their textbooks, said one RFTEN faculty member who observed her students at work. Her candidates, largely graduating seniors, were in their twelfth week of "teaching" at Dr. Carlos J. Finlay Elementary School in Miami. In preparation for their tutoring and one-on-one instruction, candidates develop nine detailed and standards-based lesson plans for writing and reading instruction that include objectives, assessments, materials used, and steps and procedures. Among the struggling readers, FIU candidates are assigned children with learning disabilities and those who are learning English as a second language. After each lesson, and at the end of the semester, students are required to write reflections that link assessment and instruction in SBRR.

When it launched the practicum experience, FIU partnered with two local public schools that served as venues for candidates to tutor. One partner school discontinued its participation as a practicum site. Another school that met the criteria to maximize the candidates' tutoring experience was identified and named as a replacement site. Today, FIU partners with Dr. Carlos J. Finlay Elementary School, a bustling and sparkling new schoolhouse that sits in the shadow of FIU's University Park Campus, which includes the College of Education. This practicum setting was chosen because the school's students collectively scored low over a period of time on Florida's mandated reading tests. The school, through the leadership of its principal, has initiated a number of interventions, including the reading practicum, designed to improve student scores. The decision to conduct the reading practicum at the school was a joint initiative by the school leadership and the university's Department of Curriculum and Instruction. The decision by the department leadership stems from the commitment to diversity held by all elements of the university. At Finlay, a Title I (Improving the Academic Achievement of the Disadvantaged) school mandated by the federal government, children participate in a dual language and literacy program where they speak and learn in English 60 percent of the day and speak and learn in Spanish for the remaining 40 percent.

Finlay's large library/media center is where FIU candidates teach and tutor. Finlay and FIU officials are reporting achievement gains among students participating in the one-on-one reading instruction. Most of the students are now at or above grade level in reading comprehension, one of the five reading components the candidates teach each week. Finlay's principal attributes much of the reading and academic success of her students to the partnership with FIU and to the placement of teacher candidates. Over time, the candidates have been able to create bonds, provide attention and continuity, and build trust with their assigned students.

Who are Finlay students? Most are immigrants, students and families who represent a transient population. Few parents speak English, and most are unable to reinforce student learning at home. According to school officials, reading is their students' "weakest link." For the majority of children, English is their second language, which often makes them struggling readers. Through the FIU practicum and clinical experience, students at Finlay gain individualized instruction that they would not receive in a classroom with more than thirty students.

On the basis of reports (school and statewide assessments) shared by the Finlay school principal and RFTEN faculty, there is evidence to suggest that the reading practicum, in combination with other reading and programmatic strategies initiated by the school, is having a significant and positive effect on reading achievement. The impact of the RFTEN model and SBRR instruction is evident in the Florida Comprehensive Assessment Test scores and in the transformation of students designated by their teachers as "critical need" students who had been retained or held back or flagged by teachers because they exhibit behavioral problems or are emergent readers.

Omar, a senior elementary education major, described his student as humorous, but "like a freight train when he gets turned on to reading. There is no stopping him. He began on a second-grade level, now he is closing the year on a third-grade level, heading for the fourth."

Morris, a 2005 FIU graduate and second-grade teacher at Finlay Elementary School, said that the clinical experience and training in SBRR are paying off for him and his students. Morris attributes his competitive edge and hire to his ability to teach reading. He came to Finlay knowing how to write a comprehensive lesson plan and how to use evidence-based reading strategies that work. Erika, also a recent FIU graduate, returned to the campus to pursue a graduate degree in reading while working as a first-year teacher. Said Erika, "When I entered the classroom I felt prepared to teach reading, I felt like I had a bag of tricks to teach reading because I had learned so much while at FIU, especially from the last and most important course, the practicum and clinical experience."

The Role of Diversity in Teacher Preparation

A strong commitment to diversity provides the foundation for the reading program delivered by the College of Education. The commitment to diversity is evidenced in the university's mission and is reflected in the enrollment of more than 34,000 students from diverse backgrounds, in new academic program initiatives, and in the delivery of programs designed to respond to the needs of the economically disadvantaged community where FIU is located. The decision to use the reading education program to promote service to economically and academically disadvantaged students is consistent with the mission of the university and the conceptual framework of the College of Education.

There was a time when dispatching FIU teacher candidates into the field meant assigning them to one of three types of schools—white, black, or Hispanic. Today, however, those types of schools no longer exist in the Miami-Dade school system, said RFTEN faculty. Responding to those changing demographics is part of the challenge that faces teacher educators at FIU in preparing teachers for diverse classrooms.

At Finlay Elementary School, immigrant children arrive almost daily to the school who are brand new to the United States. Finlay is typical of Miami's more than 200 public schools in its diverse student population. Students who used to be classified as minority today comprise the majority population in the school system. There is often an assumption that teacher candidates who had been English-language learners will be able to identify with children in their classrooms who speak their language and share the same home country. Instead, RFTEN faculty point to the "wide cultural gap" that can exist between the candidates, who are often middle-class by the time they go to college, and those children just arriving in the United States. RFTEN faculty said they are trying to bridge that gap by offering a variety of teaching and learning opportunities, including a required course called Teaching Diverse Populations and using textbooks such as *All Children Read*. All these things, said RFTEN faculty, are aimed at helping FIU candidates "become aware and in touch again . . . to let them become empathetic with that child, helping them to connect."

Can They Teach Reading?
A Study to Track First-Year Teachers

FIU teacher candidates enrolled in the fourth practicum course are not the only ones reflecting on teaching and learning. RFTEN faculty, supported by RFTEN project funds, assess their own effectiveness in preparing teachers who can teach reading. A research study launched in 2006 by one such reading faculty is examining the effect of FIU's elementary teacher preparation program by tracking how effective first-year teachers are in teaching and impacting student reading achievement. The much-anticipated findings hold the promise of providing more information on the effectiveness of SBRR and strategies for classroom reading instruction.

Ingredients for Success:
Recommendations and Lessons Learned

When the RFTEN faculty in the College of Education were asked to reflect on what makes their program and faculty team strong, the challenges they face in implementing SBRR and the RFTEN model, what strengthens their reading curriculum, and how they are working to empower their candidates, they shared these ingredients, lessons learned, and recommendations:

- Be open to collaboration.
- Network. Find strength in numbers even outside your department or institution. Seek opportunities to connect with others to create dialogues.
- Use the NCATE standards and look closely at the curriculum; expectations for the children must be high. In addition, teachers must have opportunities to know how to give the best instruction possible and to inspire children so that they can read, learn, and achieve.
- Look critically at your teacher education program. What are you doing well? What guidelines can you glean from national organizations, from the literature, from professional organizations? What can you use to improve your program?
- FIU is driven to provide the best teacher education program it can give. It is doing this by embracing change and being willing to modify, to try new things, to reflect, and to asking what worked and what did not so that effective change can be made.
- A large part of program improvement at FIU has come from looking closely at NCATE standards and saying let's assess and look at where the children are and the best ways to get them to where they need to be.
- Be very honest.
- FIU has a teacher education program that is large and includes reading faculty who work collaboratively and rely on strong graduate students, lecturers, and adjunct faculty. Size does not matter, however. The teaching and learning opportunities offered to candidates at FIU can be modeled and replicated. Keep in mind that change and new approaches often face resis-

tance and challenges, but that these can be overcome with focus and deter-mination. Such was the case with RFTEN. "The biggest resisters to implanting the project at FIU," said RFTEN faculty, "are those who feel comfortable doing business as usual or who are unable or unwilling to respond to daily demands. People not wanting to give up what they think is right." RFTEN faculty say they are meeting challenges to SBRR and RFTEN by adhering to the NCATE standards and, at the same time, help-ing to "nudge detractors along."

CHAPTER THREE

RFTEN Executive Summary and Research Implications

Preparing Effective Teachers of Reading: Putting Research Findings to Work for Student Learning

EMERSON ELLIOTT

Evaluators' summary

The Reading First Teacher Education Network (RFTEN) project changed the way teacher candidates at RFTEN institutions are taught to teach reading. Syllabi were changed to reflect scientifically-based reading research (SBRR) more fully, clinical experiences and practice teaching were created in supportive settings, RFTEN participants learned more about SBRR and related interventions, they taught what they knew to teacher candidates, candidates learned and applied SBRR-related concepts, and RFTEN participants shared their knowledge with other professionals in their community (i.e., institution colleagues and public school personnel). Change took place. In this regard, the VGCRLA resources—reading instruction expertise, training experience with institutions of higher education, a diverse array of instructional materials, and a cadre of reading consultants—were the strong substantive foundation for RFTEN.

Part of RFTEN's legacy at these partner institutions is the impressive array of courses infused with scientifically-based reading instruction, partnership arrangements that can reinforce course experiences, and, especially, newly SBRR-trained teacher candidates ready to enter America's classrooms. There is no calculation attempted here of the number of pupils whose reading skills could be immeasurably improved during the careers of these new teachers—or of others who will follow. But that impact on reading is the bottom line and it will be favorably affected as a result of RFTEN.

The evidence cited in the evaluation report shows that the RFTEN participants achieved and enjoyed significant personal and professional growth from their participation in the project. They were engaged. The teacher candidates who enrolled in RFTEN courses perceived their own advance in knowledge about the teaching of reading and in confidence of their ability to teach reading. While the evaluators would have preferred assessment evidence to corroborate the candidate perceptions, little of it was made available. Yet Bethune-Cookman College provided an exemplary illustration of assessment measures and results from their RFTEN candidates. Their submission demonstrated that appropriate assessments can be created to monitor candidate progress, and also provide compelling evidence of candidate proficiencies, in scientifically-based reading instruction.

In summary, there is compelling evidence that RFTEN did what it said it would do in the 2003 proposal.

Introduction

In the fall of 2003, the U.S. Department of Education made a grant of $4.5 million to the National Council for Accreditation of Teacher Education (NCATE) to improve reading instruction in teacher preparation programs over a three-year period. The grant, RFTEN, was supported with allocations from the secretary of education's discretionary funds. *Preparing Effective Teachers of Reading* is the final evaluation report for the three-year experience.

Two key features of the grant were its intended participants and its structure. Institutions participating in the project were to be historically black colleges and universities (HBCUs), Hispanic-serving institutions (HSIs), and tribal colleges (TCs). The grant brought a collaborative partnership together, consisting of NCATE as the awardee and manager of the project, contributing its network of contacts with colleges of education; the National Institute of Child Health and Human Development (NICHD) at the National Institutes of Health (NIH), bringing its experience and findings from the National Reading Panel (NRP) and decades of research on reading; and the University of Texas Vaughn Gross Center for Reading and Language Arts (VGCRLA), with its history of collaborative efforts to engage the higher education community in establishing research-based reading instruction in public schools.

RFTEN, like the Reading First program in the federal No Child Left Behind Act of 2001, was developed as a response to low reading scores found by the National Assessment of Educational Progress. In the 2005 reading assessment, 36 percent of all fourth-grade students scored at a "below basic" level. Among racial and ethnic minority groups, however, NAEP reported 58 percent at a below basic level for African American students, 54 percent for Hispanic students, and 52 percent for American Indian/Alaska Native students. The proposal was created to prepare effective teachers of reading for these children, as reading is the key that unlocks doors to higher-level learning. Project sponsors were certain that reading research strongly supported conclusions regarding instructional practices but realized that little would change in the classroom unless teachers were prepared to use these research findings. RFTEN would change the way that teachers were prepared to teach reading and to improve student performance by equipping teachers to use effective reading instruction practices.

The new element of RFTEN was to use scientifically based reading research (SBRR) knowledge in real-world operational settings. To carry out its work, the RFTEN proposal and the subsequent project brought together the following resources:

- Strongly supported findings from decades of research brought together by the National Reading Panel and NICHD
- Collaborative training seminars from the VGCRLA
- HEC Online, the VGCRLA Higher Education Collaborative online professional networking system
- Reading consultants for RFTEN institutions to draw from
- Extensive resources and instructional materials on SBRR from the VGCRLA
- Technical consultants, known as quality assurance coaching consultants (QACCs), whom NCATE assigned to each institution to assist in implementation and institutionalization
- Grant funds from the U.S. Department of Education
- NCATE meetings with institution presidents
- NCATE meetings with institution deans

RFTEN's contribution was to be achieved through two principal strategies. First, the project sought buy-ins from college and university presidents for both implementing the RFTEN project and realigning their reading curriculum so that scientifically based reading instruction was included. Second, RFTEN engaged and trained teacher preparation faculty so they could bring reading instruction into alignment with scientifically based reading instruction through focused professional development, guides, instructional materials, and reading consultants.

Excerpts from the RFTEN proposal have been grouped and summarized to create four statements of RFTEN purposes and objectives; these are the headings for the next section. A concluding section comprises counsel obtained from deans through survey questions requesting their advice for the RFTEN sponsors and partners and, finally, the evaluators' conclusions drawing on their experience across the life of the project and their interpretations of the data.[1]

RFTEN Purposes and Objectives

Change reading instruction for new teachers to incorporate SBRR

EXCERPTS FROM THE RFTEN PROPOSAL

Objective 1—Align teacher preparation course curricula with effective research based practices in reading;

Objective 3—Assure that professors are knowledgeable on scientifically-based reading research and are incorporating critical components of this research into teacher preparation courses;

Objective 4—Provide training materials, including the National Teacher Reading Academy developed by VGCRLA, to teacher preparation program faculty to enhance their knowledge and skills in teaching reading and language arts;

Objective 5—Establish a community of faculty, including an online community of practice, in the ongoing process of adjusting their instruction and materials to enhance the implementation of the scientifically-based reading research to better prepare teachers.

The signature activity of RFTEN was to expose faculty in participating institutions to presentations and materials on effective reading instruction and SBRR that would enlarge their own knowledge and stock of references. The professional knowledge and materials would serve as resources from which faculty would draw to revise their own syllabi and courses. Data on syllabi, courses offered, enrollments, follow-through with partnership arrangements, and continued faculty efforts to deepen their understanding of effective reading instruction are all indicators of what RFTEN has accomplished.

Courses and syllabi. When thirty-nine faculty syllabi were initially submitted for VGCRLA review in spring 2003, data collected for RFTEN indicated that SBRR findings about effective reading instruction were already in use to some extent. However, the degree of use varied, leaving room for improvement (Chapter I, Table I.1).[2] On an SBRR reading topic inclusion scale from 0 to 2, the initial median rating was 1.5; the median rating reached 1.75 after faculty revisions to incorporate SBRR-related material. The number of syllabi that reached the perfect score of 2.0 increased from seven initially to eighteen (Chapter II, Table II.1).

RFTEN institutions in Cohorts 1 and 2 modified or created 100 courses that incorporate essential elements of reading instruction from SBRR. During the

2005–2006 academic year, there were 1,751 candidate enrollments in these cours-es, and since the SBRR-revised courses have been offered, there have been a total of 3,627 candidate enrollments (Table III.1).

Field experiences. RFTEN faculty expanded and developed opportunities for can-didates to interact with students in preschool to grade 3 (P–3). As teaching is a prac-tice profession, candidates need frequent and diverse opportunities to experience teaching—explicitly, teaching that draws from SBRR. These experiences should expose candidates to increasing levels of responsibility, culminating in the practice teaching component of teacher preparation. RFTEN faculty pursued university/school partnership arrangements that allowed candidates to work direct-ly with P–3 students through tutoring and other instructional tasks in course work, in classroom settings, and, finally, in practice teaching. RFTEN could not have achieved its purpose without this contribution by the RFTEN faculty.

Institutions reported the strategies that reading faculty used to implement RFTEN, emphasizing faculty collaboration, 86 percent; faculty professional prepa-ration, 93 percent; use of the VGCRLA materials and training, 86 percent; and modification of courses to incorporate SBRR, 96 percent (Table IV.1).

Approximately 86 percent of the RFTEN institutions reported that their school partnerships were with Reading First, No Child Left Behind (NCLB) "low-performing," or other schools that use an SBRR-based reading instruction program (survey item #55, Chapter II). Institutions indicated that 14 percent of their RFTEN candidates were assigned to other schools where SBRR may not have been supported.

RFTEN faculty made substantial investments in staff development at partner schools, sharing their SBRR knowledge from the VGCRLA collaborative devel-opment seminars. These teachers (and community members also) have new knowl-edge and skills that have increased the nation's capacity for implementing effective teaching of reading based on SBRR. The eighty-six reading faculty directly trained in the RFTEN-sponsored collaborative development seminars, in turn, trained ninety-two of their colleagues, thereby more than doubling the reach of the RFTEN collaborative seminars (Chapter III, Table III.5). RFTEN institutions reported that more than 900 individuals, including 529 teachers and 388 parents, teacher aides, day care workers, and other "community members" were trained in partner schools (Chapter III, Table III.6).

Overall, it appears there was consistency between the SBRR coursework that candidates undertook in the RFTEN project and the field experiences and prac-tice teaching opportunities made available to them. The SBRR-trained partnership staff and the partners' use of SBRR reading instruction curricula made it possible to achieve this consistency.

Reading instruction materials. RFTEN faculty agreed that the collection of eighteen reading instruction materials (pamphlets, guides, videos, CDs, toolkit, models) assembled and made available by the VGCRLA was valuable and worthy of their time and effort. A faculty survey on these materials found that they had enhanced faculty participants' own knowledge of reading and how to teach it: from 82 percent to 94 percent of faculty agreed or strongly agreed (Chapter II, Table II.6). Five of the materials were used *regularly* or *occasionally* by large majorities of RFTEN faculty (80 percent to 94 percent), all of them clearly focused on teaching students in the early elementary years. Nine of the materials were ranked by RFTEN faculty between 84 percent and 90 percent for their *value* as a source of information.

Building a community of learners/teachers. The RFTEN proposal envisioned a group of faculty who were, themselves, learners and who would work collegially "in the on-going process of adjusting their instruction and materials to enhance the implementation" of SBRR in their classrooms.

One indicator of community in the project was faculty responses on uses of the VGCRLA materials described above. In a survey, faculty indicated their use or anticipated use of the materials on the basis of twenty-one statements ranging from "concern" and "need information," through "getting organized," to "leading staff development using materials this coming semester"—the latter two suggesting more serious intent (Chapter II, Table II.7). Among the choices, those indicating work with colleagues showed high levels of agreement—for example, sharing materials with other college faculty, 92 percent; leading training sessions based on the reading materials, 83 percent.

The Higher Education Collaborative (HEC) Online was one important device to encourage a community of learners/teachers. It offered Web-based collaboration with colleagues, access to materials, a base of support for including SBRR in reading instruction, a means to sustain RFTEN activities after the grant had ended, a way to stimulate thinking, and opportunities to request information. The value of HEC Online, however, was dependent on its level of use. In fact, there was very little use at all by Cohort 1 participants in the initial project year, but both Cohorts 1 and 2 averaged several hundred logins and postings for the second and third project years. The participation ranges for individual faculty members were extreme, from none to more than a hundred. The measure is "logins" or "postings," counted by the computer (Chapter II, Table II.12).

The data may just reflect the ever-enlarging but uneven growth in Web-based technology. Technology has made previously unimaginable resources accessible to all and has redefined our ideas about the form and speed of communication. It has reached some institutions and some faculty sooner than others, but its extension to all is inevitable. If RFTEN were to be proposed today, instead of in 2003, Web- and Internet-based technology would still be an integral part of the project's structure.

Build Capacity to Sustain Effective Reading Instruction

EXCERPTS FROM THE RFTEN PROPOSAL

Improve the capacity of teacher preparation programs and ensure that the changes are institutionalized;

> Objective 2—Assure that college presidents and deans are knowledgeable on scientifically-based reading research and are incorporating critical components of this research into faculty selection and evaluation.

Fundamental to implementing RFTEN was engagement of college presidents and deans, making them more knowledgeable about SBRR and supportive of its potential. The purpose was to enhance the implementation of SBRR, creating institutions that could embrace changes in faculty knowledge, resource materials, partnerships, courses, and experiences of candidates. Institutional leaders would embrace change by their building capacity (i.e., setting goals, measuring results, identifying needs for training of faculty, updating courses, etc.).

In their summary report *Analyzing the RFTEN Site Visit Reports,*[3] authors Denise Littleton and Margaret Cole White, in a separate report prepared for RFTEN, concluded that "[u]tilizing a top-down approach involving the upper administration with visits by QACCs to provide external support for project implementation appears to have been a successful strategy" (Chapter I). The summary covered reports from up to three institutional visits occurring before RFTEN's midpoint. Because the QACC reports were prepared on the basis of on-site visits, Littleton and White's summary provides a perspective on what was actually happening on RFTEN campuses that may not be evident from survey data.

At the conclusion of RFTEN, deans responded to questions about "strategies" their institution used during the RFTEN project, scored on a three-point scale: used *to a significant degree,* made *some use of this strategy,* and *did not use this strategy* (Table II.15, responses to item #81 on the spring 2006 survey). Institutions most frequently selected data systems strategies—for example, data systems making information available to faculty, 86 percent; collecting information on candidates' progress, 79 percent; and providing faculty access to records of their teacher candidates, 75 percent. However, hiring new reading faculty who know SBRR (79 percent) and budget allocations for faculty staff development (86 percent) were also frequently selected.

Deans submitted their own ideas of strategies for increasing capacity to sustain reading instruction based on sound research: six of the twenty-eight deans cited required courses and modified clinical experiences that would remain after RFTEN, four mentioned SBRR library collections that had been created and that would be retained, seven listed faculty who have been trained and recruited with SBRR knowledge, and five mentioned research grant reports that would keep the RFTEN experience accessible.

These data appear to indicate substantial, although not universal, involvement of deans and presidents in RFTEN. Presidents and deans played supporting roles and represented voices for SBRR. The data provide some support for a contention that an enhanced capacity to sustain SBRR reading instruction programs will remain after RFTEN. Both Littleton and White's analysis and the spring 2006 survey found consistently high responses to the series of questions on data system capabilities, a capacity that the Baldrige organizational performance quality program would support.[4] There seems to be an imperfect connection, however, between the availability of these data systems and the use of data when faculties make judgments about "success." The "criteria to decide" successful strategies for improving candidate SBRR learning and opportunities for practice were derived from the data infrequently.

Increase National Resources for Effective Teaching of Reading

---

EXCERPTS FROM THE RFTEN PROPOSAL

Summary statement—Increase the numbers of teachers prepared to meet the challenges of No Child Left Behind

The summary statement from the RFTEN proposal clearly indicates an intended project result: an increase in the number of teachers who can use scientifically based reading instruction in their teaching.

As noted under the heading "Courses and syllabi," during the 2005–2006 academic year, there were 1,751 candidate enrollments in the SBRR courses, and there were 3,627 candidate enrollments over the life of RFTEN (Chapter III, Table III.1). However, candidates may take two or more SBRR courses. A better approximation of the cadre of teacher candidates prepared as a result of RFTEN can be found in the number of candidates who have performed their culminating practice teaching after enrollment in SBRR courses. In total, 1,400 candidates completed practice teaching in 2005–2006, and another 1,181 completed in previous years, for an RFTEN project total of 2,589 new teacher candidates prepared with SBRR foundations. For 2005–2006, the median number of practice teaching completions was 20.5 per institution (Chapter III, Table III.2).

Ensure That Candidates Have SBRR Knowledge and Skills

EXCERPTS FROM THE RFTEN PROPOSAL

Project outcome, RFTEN proposal, pp. 14 and 15—All graduates of the participating institutions will receive a solid foundation in scientifically-based reading research and strategies to increase P–3 student achievement.

VGCRLA survey of candidate knowledge and skills. One piece of evidence that candidates increased their knowledge of SBRR and their confidence in using that knowledge was gathered from large numbers of RFTEN course completers in the 2004–2005 academic year. Candidates were asked to compare their end-of-course knowledge with their estimated beginning-of-course knowledge and also to indicate their confidence of success in using that knowledge. On the scale, a total score of forty points across ten categories represented perfect *expert knowledge*, thirty signified *considerable knowledge*, and twenty just *some knowledge* (Tables III.10 and III.11). For 835 responding undergraduates, mean scores for knowledge increased over the semester from 20.31 to 33.72, an increase of 13.41 points. Graduate student means increased from 21.63 to 34.39, or 12.76 points.

State teacher test measures of candidate knowledge. As one of the project outcomes, the RFTEN proposal included an explicit task to examine "alignment" of national tests used by states for licensure of new teachers. The intention of the examination in the context of RFTEN was to determine whether and how well any state licensure tests examine candidates' knowledge of scientifically based reading instruction—that is, the alignment of test content with the elements of effective reading instruction from SBRR. A second question was to be whether the RFTEN project might find some way to access the best-aligned test so that it could be administered as a culminating and common assessment for all RFTEN candidates. NCATE commissioned a study by Dr. Diana Rigden, now vice president of the Teacher Education Accreditation Council but a staff member of AACTE when she wrote the paper that reached the following conclusions:

- The licensure tests reviewed for this report that were developed specifically to measure a teacher candidate's knowledge of reading are generally well aligned with the essential components of effective instruction as defined by scientifically-based reading research (SBRR). Three RFTEN states measure how well candidates understand the five components of successful reading instruction—California and Virginia, which have commissioned multiple-choice tests from National Evaluation Systems (NES), and Tennessee, which has adopted the Educational Testing Service Praxis Test 0201, Reading Across the Curriculum: Elementary.

- The remaining 13 RFTEN states do not administer licensure tests that effectively measure SBRR knowledge. They (1) make no attempt to assure schools and districts that their new teachers have the training to be effective reading teachers, (2) require Praxis 0200, Introduction to the Teaching of Reading, which is not aligned with SBRR, or (3) (most often) rely on multi-subject licensure tests.

Dr. Rigden found that the frequently used multisubject tests she examined have too few items directed explicitly to the teaching of reading to provide reliable evidence and that those items are not closely aligned with the essential components of effective reading instruction as identified by SBRR.

Attempt to gather candidate assessment data on RFTEN completers. In addition to the commissioned study, the twenty-eight RFTEN Cohort 1 and 2 institutions were asked to provide candidate assessment evidence in the 2005–2006 culminating project year. The evidence was in a form that closely parallels NCATE's expectations for assessment evidence in response to its Unit Standard 1 on Candidate Knowledge, Skills, and Dispositions.

Twelve RFTEN institutions responded to the evaluators' request for assessment results about candidate knowledge, practice, and student learning effects:

- *Candidate knowledge of SBRR content*: One institution's assessment was a course requirement to define each of the five essential elements of effective reading instruction and give examples. One used course grades, two used Praxis content test results, and two included some aspect of content knowledge in a teaching portfolio. Seven of the responses included no measurement of SBRR content or submitted references too vague to summarize.
- *Candidate application of knowledge in teaching situations*: Four institutions made use of portfolios that included lesson plans and rubrics, some specific to scientifically based reading instruction; one institution reported from candidates' tutoring experiences during an SBRR course; one reported

grades in methods courses; and two used interview or observation instruments that did not incorporate any SBRR elements. Four of the twelve institutions reported nothing for this category.

- *Candidate effects on student learning:* Three institutions reported that candidates administered Dynamic Indicators of Basic Early Literacy Skills (DIBELS)[5] assessments and one made explicit reference to use of the VGCRLA "Three-Tier Model" for reading instruction, but no student learning data were provided. Three other institutions referred to "student growth" or "student learning samples," although data were either not included or not provided in a useful form. One report included testimonial letters on student progress.

One of the twelve submissions was distinguished by its responsiveness to the evaluators' request. This submission from Bethune-Cookman College incorporated content knowledge, application of knowledge, and effects on student learning measures. It included a thoughtful interpretive statement and added such illuminating touches as research references and explicit statements of what goals or standards were the bases for candidate assessments.

Understanding what NCATE means by candidate assessments and measuring candidates' progress should have been identified as a bigger challenge earlier in the life of the project. Of the twenty-eight Cohort 1 and 2 institutions, sixteen did not respond at all to the request for end-of-project candidate assessment evidence. For eleven respondents, the data were sparse or nonexistent, large areas were simply omitted, or few interpretations were provided. Bethune-Cookman College offered an exemplary response demonstrating that the task was doable and, when done well, could provide excellent evidence that RFTEN candidates were completing their programs well prepared to be effective teachers of reading based on SBRR.

Concluding Perspectives

RFTEN deans provided departing counsel to the sponsors and partners of RFTEN. They responded to questions about which elements of RFTEN worked well for them and which did not and suggested what might have been done differently to achieve greater success. Any serious evaluation must take into account the perspectives of the participants, and that is what the evaluators sought to accomplish in this portion of the report. These concluding perspectives begin with deans' observations on the RFTEN implementation strategies they employed and found successful, then turns to their advice for RFTEN sponsors and partners. The two final subsections summarize the evaluators' comments on the deans' advice and the evaluators' own observations on the RFTEN experience as a whole.

Implementation Strategies Used in RFTEN

Institutions reported the strategies used by reading faculty to implement RFTEN. They emphasized (Table IV.1): faculty collaboration, 86 percent; faculty professional preparation, 93 percent; use of the VGCRLA materials and training, 86 percent; and modification of courses to incorporate SBRR, 96 percent.

Faculty participants made their own value-added contributions to enrich the experience of teacher candidates in the RFTEN program. Five strategies were employed by institutions *to a significant degree* (Table IV.2): instruction in SBRR courses, 93 percent; arranging scientifically based reading instruction opportunities for candidates in their clinical experiences, 82 percent; candidates working one on one with students, 89 percent; candidates working with groups of low-performing students, 89 percent; and candidates working with students of differing skill levels, 89 percent. Institutions also reported frequent candidate administration of DIBELS or TPRI[6] assessments (50 percent) and new clinical and field experiences (64 percent).

Perhaps the greatest consensus was revealed when institutions responded to an invitation to identify the "one or two . . . most successful" strategies for enriching candidates' reading instruction experiences. Nine institutions listed clinical and field experiences, seven identified candidates' tutoring individual low-performing students, and three selected candidate administration of reading assessments.

Asked to list the criteria they used to judge the most successful strategies for preparation of new teachers in the use of scientifically based reading instruction, RFTEN participants described criteria that did not involve data or represented "soft" data. For example, candidates "were able to provide positive and enjoyable experiences, to implement SBRR techniques and are more open to using these." The evaluators would have been pleased to see responses indicating regular employment of strong measures and data underlying decisions made about the *most successful* strategies.

VGCRLA staff made judgments about faculty participant completion of required RFTEN activities, and these judgments serve as one indicator of RFTEN engagement. The judgments show that two of seventy-five (less than 3 percent) RFTEN faculty had completed all requirements, another forty-three (57 percent) had completed two-thirds or more of the requirements, and thirty (40 percent) had completed half or less during the second project year (Chapter II, Table II.10).

At the conclusion of the project, deans were asked to list other strategies they implemented for RFTEN in their institutions (item #72). Of those who responded, seventeen mentioned staff development for training of partnership school teachers, five listed course-based field work, and another five indicated committee and planning efforts with partner schools. Asked to list the "one or two" strategies they found most successful, eleven deans noted faculty efforts with partner schools (Table IV.1), and thirteen listed one or more of the faculty activities specific to elements of the RFTEN project as it was structured—such as faculty professional development in SBRR, materials made available by the VGCRLA, and reading instruction courses. When they were asked for the criteria they used to judge the most successful reading faculty strategies, however, deans listed few data-based measures. This finding was similar to the one reported above—that data-based measures were rarely used to identify successful strategies for preparation of new teachers.

Advice to the RFTEN Sponsors and Partners

The RFTEN project comprised at least eight distinguishable elements. Deans were asked to judge each of these (Table IV.3). Four elements earned the highest *extremely useful* ratings: VGCRLA collaborative training, almost 86 percent; NCATE quality assurance consultants, 75 percent; VGCRLA materials, more than 89 percent; and RFTEN project grants, almost 79 percent. The other RFTEN elements had somewhat lower rankings: meetings with deans were rated *extremely useful* in 71 percent of cases; reading consultants from the VGCRLA, about 61 percent; meetings with presidents, 50 percent; and the HEC Online system, just 36 percent.

In another survey question, deans addressed what the RFTEN sponsors and partners might have done differently to achieve greater success (spring 2006 survey, item #89). In total, the twenty-eight RFTEN institutions provided twenty-nine suggestions. The largest category of response focused on use of funds, which was mentioned by thirteen institutions (Appendix IV.D). Adding more collaborative training/professional development was one theme, and adding more consultant time was another. Two institutions suggested "more of a research model rather than a project model" for any future reading instruction initiative.

Seven institutions advised about goals and expectations for the project and about reporting requirements. They counseled early and complete listings of all expected data requirements and deadlines, including those for the evaluation. One institution suggested that the project "develop and provide pre- and posttests for teacher candidates." Finally, there were three comments about the RFTEN structure. One depicted the relationship between the VGCRLA and NCATE, saying it was "confusing at times," and "often times the information communicated was not the same." Another questioned NCATE's role in project operation while it "holds the power to accredit our institution's unit."

Evaluators' Views on Participants' Advice

Concluding lessons to be learned by the RFTEN project partners selected for mention here concern RFTEN's structure and management, plans for collecting data, and assessments of candidates as well as RFTEN faculty participants.

In the final evaluation survey administered in spring 2006, respondents commented on the joint roles of the VGCRLA and NCATE. Those comments touched on two issues, and this was not the first time that anyone associated with RFTEN saw or heard them expressed. One issue was a perception among participants that they received conflicting directions from the VGCRLA and from NCATE. This was another expression of an issue found in survey responses indicating that the VGCRLA reading consultants and the NCATE quality assurance coaching consultants produced confusion that seemed counterproductive. VGCRLA staff generally managed the direct day-to-day contacts with faculty participants, whereas NCATE's contacts were with deans. The partners held differing views about assessment, for example, and their separate lines of institutional contact conveyed that difference back to institutions. Given the purposes and the focal institutions for the project, RFTEN could not have been conducted by either of these partners alone. The lesson for the RFTEN partners and sponsors is that a more concerted effort should have been made to integrate the different perspectives represented by the VGCRLA and NCATE before the start of the project. Although that might have slowed the start of the project, it could have saved time and confusion later on.

A second issue, mentioned above, was raised by a respondent who questioned NCATE's role in project direction while it "holds the power to accredit our institution's unit." Such a perception is surely understandable, although it was heard infrequently as RFTEN unfolded. This is a major and continuing debate within NCATE: what is the appropriate boundary for an agency whose role is to judge whether professional educator preparation units are meeting standards, while one intention of the agency's standards is to help the profession achieve a vision of what is good and sufficient performance. NCATE has previously acknowledged (through its HBCU network project) a special responsibility to assist institutions serving populations whose members have too often been underrepresented in all aspects of American life, including teaching. Moreover, a substantial proportion of the same underrepresented populations that policymakers are seeking to recruit into teaching are prepared in the RFTEN institutions. Thus, although NCATE acknowledged the appearance of conflicting roles, their abiding interest in raising performance for institutions serving predominantly minority populations is also acknowledged.

On many occasions, RFTEN participants raised issues about data collection plans and assessments. Although the evaluation plan in the appendix to the introduction was shared with deans at their first meeting in December 2003, and again in October 2005, that information was not sufficient for all the participants. In addition, there were many periodic reporting requirements for the U.S. Department of Education and several data collections by VGCRLA, so the cumulative effect at the institutional level was probably substantial. Less clear, however, is the extent to which reporting requirements and expectations were shared between deans and their RFTEN faculty participants. Sometimes the evaluators' conversations were with faculty participants rather than with representatives of the deans or the deans themselves.

As evaluators' conversations continued during 2005 and 2006, and the assessment evidence was submitted—or not submitted, in most cases—it seemed that the RFTEN faculty may not have been as well informed about, or may not have been regular participants in, the sorts of candidate assessments that NCATE institutions are expected to use. Perhaps the information was not requested in a way that sounded similar to NCATE, although the communications with institutions all used wording that paralleled NCATE standards and reporting formats. Perhaps the institutions were not as far along in development of assessment systems as NCATE thought. Or perhaps this was an area where the differing perspectives of the VGCRLA and NCATE on assessment created confusion.

If RFTEN could be reinvented, then the advice of the evaluators is that an assessment should be identified at the outset that could be consistently administered to all completing candidates across all participating RFTEN institutions. It may also be appropriate to administer this instrument to the participating RFTEN faculty— not just for the results but to assist them in understanding what will be expected of candidates. Obvious examples for such assessments would be those required for licensure of candidates who will teach reading in California, Virginia, and Tennessee. The cost would not be incidental, and neither the difficulties of administrative arrangements nor those of securing agreement for access to such appropriate tests should be underestimated.

Notes

* The text from this chapter is taken from the Introduction from the RFTEN Final Evaluation Report Executive Summary, December 19, 2006.

1. The data that appear in this evaluation report have been compiled from numerous sources; they were provided by twenty-eight institutions that entered the project in 2003–2004 or in 2004–2005—institutions that were able to participate in the full range of RFTEN activities, including collaborative training, using materials in syllabi, revising course offerings, and field and practice teaching experiences. These are referred to as Cohorts 1 and 2. Institutions added in 2005–2006 had more limited participation, and there were no opportunities for candidates to complete courses and practice teaching before the grant expired.

2.   All references to chapters and tables are to the corresponding chapters and tables in the full volume of the RFTEN Executive Summary, *Preparing Effective Teachers of Reading: Putting Research Findings to Work for Student Learning* available on the RFTEN website (*www.rften.org*).

3.   *Analyzing the RFTEN Site Visit Reports: Inclusivity and Exemplary Reading Instruction: SBRR and the Preservice Preparation of Minority Teachers*, Denise Littleton, Professor, Norfolk State University, and Margaret Cole White, Elizabeth City, North Carolina.

4.   The Baldrige National Quality Program, issued by the National Institute of Standards and Technology (NIST), a joint public–private endeavor, fosters improved performance in organizations and corporations. Its publication "Education Criteria for Performance Excellence" provides criteria to help educational organizations—at any level, and of any size—respond to challenges; align resources and approaches; improve communication, productivity, and effectiveness; and achieve strategic goals. The U.S. Department of Commerce, NIST, administers an annual award program for institutions meeting the criteria.

5.   An assessment used to determine the need for supplemental instruction and to monitor student progress.

6.   Texas Primary Reading Inventory, an alternative to DIBELS for benchmark assessment purposes but not for frequent progress monitoring.

Increasing the Social Capital of Underrepresented Populations

ROSUSAN D. BARTEE

Institutions of higher education and public schools have a collective responsibility to close the academic achievement gap. K–16 collaborations in RFTEN changed how education is delivered to and received by its constituents. Social capital, which comprises networks and associations through which resources are made accessible, is critical to the quest to build institutional capacity (the foundational basis for which material and/or nonmaterial tools are generated to support administrative and/or programmatic activities) that becomes useful in collaborations (Arriaza, 2001; Brown & Davis, 2001; Lee & Croninger, 1999). According to a report submitted to the U.S. Department of Education (2003), programs such as RFTEN have extended beyond their demands of restructuring teacher education programs through content-specific matters and have demonstrated efforts involving the building of social capital for the participating institutions. It is specifically these social capital building efforts that contribute to the sustainability of RFTEN goals in multifaceted ways.

Establishing systems to foster social capital via a K–16 implementation model is important for equipping public school, colleges, and universities to increase their educational competitiveness. Access to different types of social capital is fundamental to the quality of resources, information, and relationships. Part of the challenge is that many individuals do not understand how networks can maximize opportunities in education. Resources (material and nonmaterial) and networks (internal and external) gained in RFTEN have provided the context in which to build capacity within these minority-serving institutions. Although RFTEN was an implementation project, it embedded research perspectives that deserve critical probing for their implications for teacher education and the general higher education community.

Background on RFTEN

In 2003, RFTEN was launched as a $4.5-million joint venture between the National Council for Accreditation of Teacher Education (NCATE), the National Institutes of Child Health and Human Development (NICHD), and the Vaughn Gross Center for Reading and Language Arts (VGCRLA) at the University of Texas at Austin.[1] Funded by the U.S. Department of Education using the secretary of education's discretionary funds, RFTEN engaged executive administrators, deans, and faculty from historically black colleges and universities (HBCUs), Hispanic-serving institutions, and tribal colleges.[2] RFTEN focused on changing reading curricula within teacher education programs by training faculty using scientifically based reading research (SBRR). These higher education faculty then train their preservice teachers in SBRR. When the preservice teachers enter into a classroom, they are prepared with research-based pedagogy and content to teach elementary students.

RFTEN had institutional buy-in from college and university presidents. The deans were responsible for the on-site administrative and implementation components of the project. Quality assurance coaching consultants (QACCs) and reading specialists provided high levels of expertise in administrative and content matters. The QACCs informed deans about the structural makeup of teacher education programs, and the reading specialists addressed the corresponding pedagogical and curriculum areas with faculty. Presidents, deans, and faculty also received professional development through various venues convened by NCATE or during national and international conferences or meetings. Each of the departments or schools of education was required to partner with a low-performing, hard-to-staff, Reading First school. These school partnerships provided the clinical venue for student teachers and early incorporation of the SBRR tenets and served as a feeder program for SBRR-trained preservice teachers.

In addition, the RFTEN project extended the Higher Education Collaborative (HEC) model as technical support to reading and special education faculty members who prepare preservice teachers across the nation. Faculty and preservice teachers had unlimited access to this online community of reading and other educational experts. Furthermore, RFTEN provided professional development forums for selected reading faculty members to be trained in SBRR. Faculty were required to attend a series of intensive SBRR training sessions conducted by reading experts affiliated with the VGCRLA. As a result, faculty were exposed to the knowledge of national experts in reading and to a venue for building professional networks and relationships.

Tenets of Educational Change, Organizational Culture, and Social Capital

To understand the dynamics of the RFTEN project as an implementation model, we must consider educational change, organizational culture, and social capital. The RFTEN project operated through top-down leadership according to theoretical perspectives on educational change (Fullan & Stiegelbauer, 1991; Joyce, Weil, & Showers, 1992). Educational change suggests that the structural components of educational policies influence the quality of educational practices and outcomes. Administrators are key in developing policies to govern colleges and are critical to the sustainability of those policies. The impact of RFTEN is evident in terms of the level of participation in required activities and collaborative efforts on and between campuses. Given that educational change occurs as a process and over a period of time, as a programmatic initiative, RFTEN provided the context to influence the ideologies and infrastructure that shape a campus community.

Organizational culture was important for the RFTEN project. Taking the pulse of an organization is critical to how programmatic activities are implemented and accepted within the institutional setting (Brown, 2000; Kuh & Whitt, 2000; Parker, 2000). According to Hill and Jones (2001), organizational culture is

> the specific collection of values and norms that are shared by people and groups in an organization and that control the way they interact with each other and with stakeholders outside the organization. Organizational values are beliefs and ideas about what kinds of goals members of an organization should pursue and ideas about the appropriate kinds or standards of behavior organizational members should use to achieve these goals. (pp. 10–11)

Each organization has an embedded culture of traditions and expectation that, in effect, impacts the interactions of the people and the quality of the relationships within the respective context. According to Hill and Jones (2001), organizational culture has the following tenets:

> From organizational values develop organizational norms, guidelines or expectations that prescribe appropriate kinds of behavior by employees in particular situations and control the behavior of organizational members towards one another. (pp. 10–11).

The organizational culture extends to certain accompanying behavioral patterns. Organizations become associated with specific dispositions that are not necessarily acceptable in other, similar contexts.

Social capital is an important component in establishing quality networks that return useful resources and relationships. Social capital gains its legitimacy and the extent of its value according to the context in which it is exchanged and/or gained. Brown and Davis (2001) assert:

> Although educational institutions can generate social capital for their students, social resources or ties can only be acquired through an individual's attendance at a particular college or university. Institutional social capital is used to distinguish it from the social ties represented by non-university friends, family members, and other resources that provide private social capital. Clearly, Black colleges disseminate particular social resources to their students and graduates. (p. 42)

HBCUs provide access to social capital networks that may not be available in other contexts. HBCUs offer the opportunity to make connections that can be transferred into financial and/or material resources. Such resources become critical to the level of social or economic stability.

Arriaza (2001) explores the contextual setting which generates social capital. The author considers social capital as involving the capacity of individuals and groups to negotiate social borders and institutional barriers. Such capacity is constructed via social networks and the intervention of protective agents. Having this built-in covering, or security, provides the assurance of disposable resources being plentiful and within reach. Social capital enables individuals to interact freely, given that their relationship is linked to their affiliation with an institution as an external, existing network. Lee and Croninger (1999) situate social capital as a "resource embedded within a person's social network . . . the manner in which the structural characteristics of social groups facilitate or hinder helpful exchanges between members" (p. 6).

Conceptual Framework

Now we examine RFTEN as an implementation model that was used to (re)produce and maintain social capital. The level of support afforded by social capital served to bind the relationships involved. According to Davis (2001):

> The concept of social support is the subject of considerable attention and research effort among social and behavioral scientists. Social bonds, social integration, and primary

group relations have long been central concepts in sociological theory and analysis. (p. 143)

These relationships may be thought of as the basic building blocks of social structure; their formation, maintenance, and severance are universal and fundamental social processes. In effect, social support provides the context in which relationships and networks operate and can be assessed.

This chapter uses document analysis as its methodological tool. Selected transcripts of the various activities associated with the RFTEN project since its implementation in 2003 are reviewed. These activities include convened meetings, seminars, and workshops and task force endeavors. The documents are viewed from the perspective of social capital, educational change, and organizational culture. Emerging themes and relevant data are identified to demonstrate how RFTEN operated in terms of social capital.

RFTEN and educational leadership

RFTEN subscribed to the use of collaborative efforts in its leadership role. The support from the administration to the practitioner became fundamental to its capacity-building efforts and to the delivery of content-specific training. The approach that RFTEN assumed was critical to public school and higher education communities. Traditional camps have sought to maintain separate organizational and governance structures for these communities (Brown, 2000). Such an approach has complicated the dialogue about who is responsible for closing the achievement gap. Is it the public schools? Is it teacher education programs within institutions of higher education? Is it society at large? One of the executive stakeholders associated with the RFTEN project asserts the following:

> There is a void in educational leadership. By that I don't mean leadership in the schools or in the school districts, but leadership that says that education is an important issue for the nation and recognizes that closing the achievement gap is the civil rights issue of our time. This is what we should be spending our energy on. (RFTEN interview, August 2006)

The argument suggests that the achievement gap is linked to the quality of educational leadership. Educational leadership sets the tone for prioritizing issues and assessing remedies in given contexts. In effect, the involvement of leaders within the RFTEN model of collaboration was a step toward changing the education process to close the achievement gap. Another executive administrator offers this perspective:

I heard the comment made earlier today about coming in and sitting around the table because if you're not at the table you might be on the menu. Well, I say something else to you—that you really have to be at the table and to partake of the meal. And I think many of us for so long have not been around the table, but as leaders you are here. You're sitting around the table, but you have some input into this menu that we are providing to you as part of our partnership, but also you're the ones who are going to see that this menu is delectable. You are the ones who are going to see that this menu is enjoyed. (RFTEN presidential advisory meeting, February 2, 2004)

Leaders with access to such fora can influence the course of educational leadership. Social capital becomes evident in the voices that are considered legitimate for offering input or responding to issues about educational leadership.

RFTEN's collaborative efforts between public schools and higher education provided a framework for educational leadership. According to one of the executive stakeholders:

RFTEN has been able to offer principles, strategies, and recommendations by equipping teacher educators and ultimately classroom teachers with tools to learn and implement scientifically based reading. In the past, we assumed that teaching reading was easy, but we know from the research conducted by NICHD, the National Reading Panel, and others that it is not. Training preservice teachers is part of the leverage needed to transform reading education and impact classroom learning. (RFTEN interview, August 2006)

This statement suggests that the quality of educational leadership is determined by the type of approaches used to address recurring problems. In its use of scientifically based research, RFTEN's framework of professional development and technical support addressed the specific issues of teacher quality that have impacted the achievement gap. Nevertheless, the identification of specific pedagogical and content approaches was not without its challenges. Issues emerged about the type of research strategies as well as the proponents or opponents of the selected strategies. An executive stakeholder asserts:

[RFTEN's] purpose—as I understand it—the only one that's been funded multiple years to work with reading faculty on your campus who teach in elementary of early childhood education—is to work with them in incorporating scientifically based reading research into their delivery of reading instruction to those majors. That is the purpose. It doesn't come without heat, if you will. There are schools or camps that don't subscribe to SBRR, but you all have said, as college presidents we've got to do something. As the Secretary said, read to learn, learn to read. It is core to everything that we do. It's not just teacher education. We might start there. (RFTEN interview, August 2006)

Although stakeholders had an interest in the welfare of higher education and public schools, they were not necessarily wedded to any one approach to improving the delivery and receipt of education. As the statements above suggest, RFTEN contended with various opinions about its pedagogical and content delivery. RFTEN's framework for educational leadership stemmed from a research basis that does not take into account the origin of the opinions.

RFTEN as a platform for convening multiple stakeholders

The RFTEN project was able to include multiple stakeholders to support its mission. This increased the quantity and quality of influential stakeholders who were exposed to and understand the vast potentials and diverse implications of RFTEN. According to one of the state directors in Reading First:

> One of the things that I said to Boyce [project director] was this is fabulous work that you are planning. It's important nationally, it's important for children that are in our schools. It's important to state superintendents of schools, the chiefs in our state education agencies, and it's important to their staffs. (RFTEN Reading First state directors meeting, May 20, 2005)

That the RFTEN project was an asset to stakeholders on the federal, state, and local levels suggests that it extended the boundaries of programmatic activities. RFTEN as a policy mechanism has implications for public education and institutions of higher education and for other, secondary but critical, stakeholders. As a macropolicy mechanism (i.e., No Child Left Behind), RFTEN contributed to rules or regulations for how to improve academic achievement; it also provided the policy context for determining how micropolicy issues (i.e., collaborative efforts between multiple stakeholders) influence or manifest within the pursuit of academic achievement. RFTEN's social capital emanated from its usefulness as a programmatic activity, which becomes evident through the buy-in of multiple influential stakeholders.

The role of RFTEN as a venue for convening multiple stakeholders was also based upon its leadership capacity. The Reading First state director quoted above specifically mentions a discussion with the RFTEN project director. Having capable and competent individuals serving in leadership positions in RFTEN was critical. In effect, building capacity using social capital became synonymous with the leadership's capacity to attract members and garner buy-in from diverse communities with similar interests. While many of the networks may be established ones, the ability to form new relationships and networks is equally important.

The RFTEN implementation model served to bridge gaps between institutions of higher education (i.e., colleges, universities) and agencies of higher education (i.e.,

Reading First programs). Although some gaps may be intentional and some may be unavoidable, gaps between similar interests offer an opportunity to engage efforts to address them. RFTEN, by focusing on reading and teacher preparation, provided a cause for colleges and universities and state agencies to unite around. According to a Reading First state director:

> I think the second thing is this RFTEN project and us—we've got to become really partners. Example—all of the Reading First grants require a state reading leadership team. Well we have the reading faculty at Alabama State on our policy committee. Every state needs to do that that RFTEN has done. I'd like to be on your project board or one of our faculty members, because that way when we do something together, we're going to get to know each other, and know how to work together. (RFTEN Reading First state directors meeting, May 20, 2005)

RFTEN provided a critical framework for dialogue and relationship building between institutions and agencies. The integration of RFTEN ideas with those of Reading First provided the overlap of interests necessary to convene in such ways that shared goals could be acquired. In effect, quality networks emerged through RTFEN's initial steps toward collaborative outreach.

RFTEN as a pathway to institutional excellence

In the era of No Child Left Behind, institutions of higher education and public schools must find ways to improve educational outcomes. For colleges and universities, achievement of such goals is often complicated by the tendency to engage in various activities and strategies that do not reflect their current expertise levels or knowledge base. Simultaneously, public schools are being overwhelmed with the implementation of diverse teaching strategies to increase educational outcomes. Teachers are required to use many different instructional approaches within their lesson plans or else face the possibility of punitive consequences if their students do not meet yearly performance requirements—not to mention that teachers are underpaid and the increased load exacerbates the reality of this salary deficit.

RFTEN offered a way to tackle some of the challenges that public schools and institutions of higher education are facing. For minority-serving institutions, RFTEN presented the opportunity to engage in the structured delivery of academic preparation in ways specific to their mission statements. HBCUs have a long tradition of teacher preparation; they have trained more than half (53 percent) of the African American teachers in public schools today (RFTEN proposal, p. 2). An executive stakeholder associated with the RFTEN project asserts:

HBCUs are vital to the nation. They have served wonderfully and have a proud history. Through RFTEN, HBCUs, Tribal Colleges, and Hispanic-serving institutions have been exposed to the more current research on evidence-based reading strategies. RFTEN has also provided access to the leading experts in the field of reading and for many of the faculty at the minority-serving institutions, the limited access to resources does not permit many of them to experience this professional luxury. Just as MIT and similar institutions have come to be known as places to go for studying science, medicine or technology, these RFTEN institutions can likewise corner the higher education market when it comes to reading and teacher education. (RFTEN interview, August 2006)

RFTEN allowed HBCUs to reaffirm their position within the higher education community. It provided up-to-date training in proven strategies in reading. The modest financial and material support that RFTEN offered institutions was useful toward effecting quality professional development.

More specifically, given that a culture often exists within institutions, RFTEN provided a venue where the needs of the school partnerships could be addressed in ways that are particular to that partnership. An executive administrator from one of the participating institutions asserts:

> This institution is something called the urban educational corridor; it is a rich K–16 model. And in essence what we are trying to do is capture children from the point of conception and move in quickly through high school . . . the network is pretty much set. So looking at the commitment we have a true K–16 model which is a very rich educational component and tool that we are pushing on our campus. (RFTEN task force meeting, April 21, 2005)

This institution of higher education has positioned itself according to the demands of the public school community. The teacher education program can be tailored to provide activities that address the ongoing and recurring issues for pre-service teachers who are fulfilling clinical practice requirements (i.e., student teaching) in those schools. Furthermore, as another executive administrator from a participating institution asserts:

> There is an excitement about the program there that I can't, you know, explain in words, so you would have to come down and see our faculty and our students involved in it to the—well, to the extent that they have sent me out to some of the schools to read to the students and we have developed our own program—very strong program there that is known throughout the campus. So our commitment is to make sure that this program and this research-based reading initiative is in place and serving the students that we are teaching as—that we are training as teachers to go out into the world to work and we are excited about that. (RFTEN task force meeting, April 21, 2005)

The gap that exists between the two communities—public schools and higher education—is bridged through efforts that appear to be initiated by the university. Social capital is gained through the access that schools have to university faculty who can serve as coaches in the efforts to enhance student achievement.

RFTEN Social Capital as Capacity Building

RFTEN as an implementation model has provided a context for generating quality networks and establishing relationships that yield both material and nonmaterial resources. From a material resource perspective of social capital, focusing on improving teacher quality via content delivery of SBRR demonstrates the efforts of minority-serving institutions to address macrolevel educational issues using microlevel approaches in educational processes. Through established partnerships with higher education agencies (i.e., NCATE, NICHD) and collaborations with schools and universities (i.e., VGCRLA), theoretically and practically sound strategies have been implemented.

From a nonmaterial resource perspective of social capital, RFTEN's capacity building engaged and solidified buy-in among the college and university presidents. Such buy-in legitimated the project as a campus-based initiative, and the campus executive buy-in changes the negotiating position about RFTEN ideals among other policy and administrative stakeholders. Access to certain groups and people who impact educational policies and practices is something that RFTEN afforded. The findings about RFTEN's social capital have raised questions for research consideration. Some research questions and corresponding goals for consideration are laid out in Table 1.

Table 1. Research Questions and Corresponding Goals for Consideration

Research Questions	Research Goals
What are the implications of targeted implementation programs within minority-serving institutions largely for higher education?	—To examine the implications of identifiable RFTEN strategies of institutional change —To assess the goals and academic outcomes of RFTEN and similar programmatic initiatives in selected minority-serving and non-minority-serving institutions —To determine the role of accreditation in implementation programs for minority-serving and non-minority-serving institutions

Table continued on next page.

How do specialized curriculum and pedagogical approaches impact students and teachers?	—To examine the effects on students in elementary school settings who have been taught by former teacher candidates trained in SBRR —To determine the correlation between SBRR training and ability to pass state licensure exams —To assess the impact of teachers trained in SBRR who are or are not teaching in their respective content areas
How does the restructuring of teacher education programs impact faculty in their classroom settings and the larger institutional context?	—To examine how programmatic initiatives affect the development and implementation of relevant policies and practices in administrative and faculty capacities —To determine whether the restructuring of teacher education programs (particularly in reading) impacts other academic disciplines
What are the implications of top-down (presidents to education deans to faculty) programmatic efforts to build institutional capacity and enhance academic outcomes?	—To assess the role of executive leadership in programmatic efforts at minority-serving and non-minority-serving institutions —To identify the different components of institutional capacities and their relationship to academic outcomes
How do partnerships between higher and public education impact the performance of students in school?	—To determine the academic impact of collaboration between institutions of higher education and low-performing/Reading First schools —To examine the outcomes of students in elementary school settings who have been taught by former teacher candidates trained in SBRR —To assess whether having targeted programs (i.e., SBRR) allows institutions to impact the outcomes of students in school.

The questions and goals listed in Table 1 enable discussion of research perspectives related to the RFTEN project. RFTEN's implementation model, combining the theoretical and practical bases for collaboration, raised critical questions that need to be addressed by the academic research and policy community. The findings will contribute to our understanding of the integration of research-based and implementation-based projects.

RFTEN demonstrated its social capital in its infrastructural capacity-building efforts through its framework for educational leadership, platform for convening multiple stakeholders, and pathway to institutional excellence. The educational leadership framework requires teacher training and teaching to be informed by research-based approaches that the field of higher education can provide. RFTEN's educational leadership platform established the need to involve diverse stakeholders. In effect, stakeholder buy-in enhanced the legitimacy of RFTEN's goals and its potential impact as an active model of social capital on multiple policy and practice arenas.

Notes

1. For the third and final year of the project, given the need to allocate resources for the RFTEN project efficiently and to implement SBRR effectively within teacher education reading courses, the VGCRLA did not continue as a partner. The former project manager of RFTEN from the VGCRLA continued as an independent consultant, performing many of the administrative functions that had been previously handled by the VBCRLA (e.g., identifying and scheduling reading specialists for site visits). Many reading specialists from the center also continued in their roles as experts for the RFTEN project. NCATE and NICHD continued as the contractors for RFTEN throughout the duration of the project. NCATE remained the primary liaison between the RFTEN project and the presidents and deans.
2. It is important to note that although the RFTEN project uses the five components of reading instruction via SBRR that Reading First grants support, RFTEN is distinct from Reading First. RFTEN focuses on both institutions of higher education and public schools through collaborative efforts to close the achievement gap.

References

Allen, W. R., E. G. Epps, & N. Haniff. (Eds.). (1991). *College in black and white: African American students in predominantly white and in historically black public universities.* New York: State University of New York Press.

Arriaza, G. (2001, April). Crime and punishment: Social capital and children of color. Paper presented at the Annual Meeting of the American Educational Research Association, Seattle, WA.

Brown. M. C. (Ed.). (2000). *Organization and governance in higher education,* 5th ed. Upper Saddle River, New Jersey: Pearson Education.

Brown, M. C. & J. E. Davis. (2001). The historically black college as social contact, social capital, and social equalizer. *Peabody Journal of Education, 76,* 31–49.

Davis, R. (2001). Social support networks and undergraduate student academic-success-related outcomes: A comparison of black students on black and white campuses. In W. R. Allen, E. G. Epps, & N. Haniff. (Eds), *College in black and white: African American students in predominantly white and in historically Black public universities* (pp. 143–157). New York: State University of New York Press.

Fullan, M. & S. Stiegelbauer. (Eds.). (1991). *The new meaning of educational change.* New York: Teachers College.

Hill, C. W. L. & G. R. Jones. (2001). *Strategic management,* 5th ed. Boston, Massachusetts: Houghton Mifflin.

Joyce, B., M. Weil, & B. Showers. (1992). *Models of teaching.* Boston: Allyn & Bacon.

Kuh, G. D. & E. J. Whitt. (2000). Culture in American colleges and universities. In M. C. Brown (Ed.), *Organization and governance in higher education* (pp. 160–169). Upper Saddle River, New Jersey: Pearson Education.

Lee, V. E. & R. G. Croninger. (1999). Elements of social capital in the context of six high schools. (Report No. EA 031052). Washington, DC: Office of Educational Research and Improvement. (ERIC Reproduction Service no. ED 454 582.)

Parker, M. (2000). *Organizational culture and identity.* London: Sage.

Preparing highly qualified teachers to leave no child behind: The Reading First Teacher Preparation Reading Excellence Network Initiative. (2003, September 3). Submitted and accepted proposal to the U.S. Department of Education in Washington, DC.

RFTEN Findings

Licensure Tests
and Effective Reading Instruction

DIANA W. RIGDEN

Reading Matters

Those involved in RFTEN know well the stark realities announced by the 2005 National Assessment of Educational Progress (NAEP) reading assessment. NAEP defines the "basic" level of reading as partial mastery of fundamental skills and knowledge, and it reported that 33 percent of U.S. fourth graders read at this level. Another 38 percent of fourth graders in the United States read at a "below basic" level. In eight of the sixteen RFTEN states, the percentage of 9-year-olds reading at a below basic level exceeds this national average.

The National Assessment of Adult Literacy report, issued in 2005, identified "Level 3" on a prose scale as the proficiency required for high-growth occupations and the minimum standard for success in today's labor market. It found that only half of the U.S. population aged 16 to 65 have reached Level 3 in reading.

The U.S. crisis in reading skills has been reported for decades. However, effective action to ensure every child learns to read has, all too frequently, been slow, halting, or missing.

It is quite likely—indeed, even probable—that candidates can be licensed to teach elementary students today without demonstrating their proficiency in essential reading instruction knowledge and skills derived from scientifically based reading research (SBRR). This assertion is warranted by evidence that only three of sixteen RFTEN states require prospective teachers to pass licensure tests that examine knowledge of effective reading practice based on sound research.

A gap is apparent between the aim of the federal Reading First grant program—that elementary students learn to read proficiently—and state practices found in standards and licensure for new elementary teachers. If teaching reading skills were a state priority, it would be reflected in state Reading/English Language Arts standards for K–4 students and state licensure requirements for elementary teachers. Yet only seven of the sixteen RFTEN states have adopted student standards aligned with effective reading instruction as identified by SBRR. And only three RFTEN states—California, Virginia, and Tennessee—have licensure tests that assure them that elementary teachers who pass have knowledge and instructional skills informed by SBRR and the National Reading Panel report of 2000.

The National Council for Accreditation of Teacher Education's (NCATE's) concern about this state of affairs led it to develop the RFTEN project. I was asked by RFTEN to look specifically at state licensure tests in reading to determine how well these tests align with the components of effective reading instruction identified by SBRR.

The Baseline for What Teachers Need to Know and to Be Able to Do

In 2000, the National Reading Panel issued a report describing five components, each strongly supported by research, essential in teaching children to read. Although these are not the only things a teacher needs to know and to be able to do, they are the baseline that every teacher must be able to master cold—the content teachers must know and be able to teach:

1. *Phonemic awareness*: the ability to teach children to focus on and manipulate phonemes (the smallest units of spoken language) in spoken syllables and words. Phonemic awareness and letter knowledge are the best predictors of how well children will learn to read during the first two years of school.
2. *Phonics*: teaching young readers explicitly and systematically to understand how letters are linked to sounds (phonemes) to form letter-sound correspondences, to recognize spelling patterns, and to apply this knowledge in reading.
3. *Reading fluency*: offering beginning readers repeated opportunities for guided oral reading to promote better word recognition, fluency, and comprehension.

4. *Vocabulary development*: helping young readers increase their vocabulary knowledge through direct and indirect teaching, with repetition and multiple exposures to vocabulary items.

5. *Reading comprehension*: teaching comprehension skills explicitly by demonstrating, explaining, modeling, and implementing specific cognitive strategies to help beginning readers derive meaning from both literary and nonliterary texts by intentional, problem-solving, thinking processes.

Preparing New Teachers to Teach Reading

To be effective in teaching children to read, classroom teachers need to know how students learn to read, how to teach students to read, how to judge how well students read, and how to strengthen students' reading skills. These four areas—acquisition, instruction, assessment, and remediation—subsume a number of other topics, including understanding what motivates students to read, differentiating instruction to students according to their varying needs, and selecting reading materials and making assignments that will encourage students to read. Teacher education programs are encouraged to educate teacher candidates in the conceptual foundations of the reading process (including the historical evolution of English, phonological awareness, and reading research) and in linguistics and the structure of language. In addition, candidates need supervised practice in teaching reading which includes opportunities to become proficient in fostering phonemic awareness and teaching letter name and shape recognition; introducing regular sound-symbol patterns, letter clusters, and syllable types; and promoting knowledge of word meanings and vocabulary development, among other things.

Reading Licensure Tests
and What Teachers Need to Know

To examine how well teacher licensure tests align with reading research, I engaged the help of Joan Sedita, a recognized reading expert, author, and teacher trainer. We reviewed the Educational Testing Service (ETS) "Test at a Glance" Web site information, expanded test specifications, and an actual instrument for each of the following teacher licensure tests in the Praxis series:

- *Elementary Education: Curriculum, Instruction, and Assessment* (0011)
- *Elementary Education: Content Knowledge* (0014)
- *Introduction to the Teaching of Reading* (0200)

- *Reading Across the Curriculum: Elementary* (0201)
- *Middle School English Language Arts* (0049)

We also reviewed test specifications and sample test information for three reading licensure tests developed by the National Evaluation Systems (NES) specifically aligned to teaching standards in three states:

- The Massachusetts *Foundations of Reading (PreK–6)*, test 90
- California's Reading Instruction Competence Assessment (RICA): *Test Information and Sample Written Examination Form* (2002)
- The Virginia Reading Assessment for Elementary and Special Education Teachers (2004)

We found that licensure tests developed specifically to measure a teacher candidate's knowledge of reading instruction are generally well aligned with the essential components of effective instruction derived from SBRR. The multiple-choice items on the three state reading licensure tests developed through the NES explicitly measure how well a candidate understands the five components of successful reading instruction. The multiple-choice items on Praxis Test 0201, *Reading Across the Curriculum: Elementary*, developed by the Educational Testing Service, are aligned with SBRR. In contrast, Praxis Test 0200, *Introduction to the Teaching of Reading*, is not aligned with SBRR findings.

This means that if licensure tests are the public assurance of teacher knowledge, then only four of the licensure tests we reviewed, three of them in RFTEN states, can serve to assure citizens that elementary teachers who pass them know how to teach reading following SBRR findings. Only Massachusetts, California, and Virginia, through their own state-specific tests, and Tennessee, which requires Praxis Test 0201, are able to assure schools and districts that their new teachers have the training to be effective reading teachers. Most states require future elementary teachers to take multisubject licensure tests that have few items directed explicitly at the teaching of reading (too few to serve as a valid measure), and those items are not closely aligned to the essential components of effective reading instruction as identified by SBRR.

Recommendations from This Analysis

Good reading skills are the necessary foundation for a productive and satisfying life, and it is the responsibility of educators to ensure that every individual learns to read. That being the case, every measure at our disposal should be used to ensure that teachers have the knowledge and skills they need to be successful reading teachers. States have an opportunity to align their education standards, requirements for teacher preparation programs, and licensure tests so that every teacher will be highly qualified in reading instruction. NCATE has an opportunity, through its standards and review processes, to guide and influence the quality of teacher preparation programs in the United States. Teaching reading effectively must be an instructional priority.

Note

To read the full report, *On Licensure Alignment with the Essential Components of Effective Reading Instruction*, visit http://www.RFTEN.org.

CHAPTER FOUR

Project Implementation and the Role of Technology

LINDA COLBURN

Goals and Intention of HEC Online

For more than a decade, computer-mediated communication (CMC) has been employed for use with kindergarten to grade 12 (K–12) teachers; its use in higher education has been greatest in distance-learning courses, where students use the discussion areas to communicate with one another and with course instructors. The RFTEN online community was not tied to an institution or course of instruction; rather it provided faculty from historically black colleges and universities, Hispanic-serving institutions, and tribal colleges with a forum for discussions related to reading instruction and research.

The Higher Education Collaborative (HEC) was established in 2000 to engage teacher educators in the discussion and implementation of scientifically based reading research (SBRR). The HEC began with a group of fifteen faculty members from colleges and universities in the state of Texas. It was a cooperative effort between the Texas Education Agency and the University of Texas Center for Reading and Language Arts, now known as the Vaughn Gross Center for Reading and Language Arts (VGCRLA). HEC Online was developed in 2003 to address Texas teacher educators' need for a forum where they could collaborate, share information and artifacts, ask questions, and communicate with one another about reading and reading instruction.

The RFTEN grant used an online community to support the professional development of teacher educators in the area of SBRR. It also provided opportunities for educators from institutions in various states and regions to collaborate and support each other in providing reading instruction and teaching. More than one hundred members at thirty RFTEN institutions had the opportunity to participate in HEC Online.

Implementation

Use of HEC Online by RFTEN members began in 2004 with the project's first cohort of partner institutions. The National Council for the Accreditation of Teacher Education (NCATE) authored the RFTEN grant, which was funded by the U.S. Department of Education. NCATE joined resources with the VGCRLA and in so doing was able to leverage resources and participate in HEC Online. RFTEN members were added to the HEC Online database, and a community was established that was accessible only to RFTEN members. In addition, RFTEN and Texas HEC members could interact across discussion forums on assessment, instruction, SBRR, and special education. Although the architecture of the site was not designed specifically with the RFTEN organization in mind, over time features such as document sharing and "Ask an Expert" were added to HEC Online to support the growing needs of members.

Members were given small stipends for actively participating in the online community. Participants were required to log in to the online community four times a month, to post responses, feedback comments, or shared documents for a total of forty topics. Member participation at the stipend level typically hovered at 42 percent for 2005 and 54 percent for 2006. Members were not compensated simply for logging in, but we found that many members logged in multiple times during the year without ever posting anything.

HEC Online Features

Initially, threaded discussions were the primary function of the site. A library was added (although it proved to be less useful than anticipated because of a perceived conflict of interest if members identified specific books and publishers), as was a place for uploading or downloading labeled shared documents. The shared documents feature proved to be especially popular and helpful, allowing faculty members to post activities, handouts, and syllabi, get feedback, and easily share documents. When both Texas and RFTEN users expressed concern over the inability to edit their own submissions, a post-submission editing feature was added to discussions. This allowed the author of the post to go back at any time and edit their topic or response. A "special education" discussion forum was added at the request of several community members.

Features were added to improve navigation and use of the site, such as flags to identify topics with new responses and email notification, which enabled members to request that they be emailed if anyone responded to their topic, helping decrease the wait-time for learning about a posted response. A "search" feature was added that allowed users to locate discussions, people, or shared documents using multiple terms. In the spring of 2006, HEC Online hosted its first "Ask an Expert" discussion, where a reading expert responded to questions and comments from community members.

Facilitating the Online Community

The facilitator's role was "being there to do everything to encourage and support participation, while doing nothing to get in the way of it." RFTEN members could email the facilitator directly for help in accessing any part of the online community. Help sessions were hosted by the facilitator at all RFTEN seminars to provide members with "hands-on" help with logging in, posting, sharing documents, and troubleshooting access problems. User guides with screenshots and step-by-step instructions were handed out at seminars and electronically posted in shared documents.

The facilitator also monitored the site, watching for responses to members' questions. If the facilitator saw that a question was not receiving attention, he or she might post a response or send out an email request to another member with the expertise to respond. In addition, the facilitator often referred posters to others who might have the resources they required.

Participation in HEC Online

Many of RFTEN's partner institutions have small education programs, and often faculty members have few colleagues in their content area. The HEC Online community provided these members with an opportunity to network with others who had similar professional interests, engage in discussion, and develop collaborative initiatives.

HEC Online had professional impact for the RFTEN members. One RFTEN faculty member reported that "HEC Online has helped me to grow." Another stated in an interview, "I don't know what I would do without HEC Online." There were also efforts to support professional collaboration. Faculty from Texas HEC and from the RFTEN project were engaged in writing a book that compiled literacy activities intended to benefit teacher educators as well as preservice and in-service teachers. Others discussed how important it was for them to have the opportunity to collaborate online:

> [We] were just discussing the benefits of sharing and discussing issues with everyone online. I've found some very interesting ideas that I can't wait to implement with my students.

> I think we realize that we are blessed to have a means of keeping in touch with so many wonderful educated people that have so much in common with us and have such an important mission.

RFTEN members frequently posted requests for information about Web sites or other resources to help with course instruction. They would also request assistance with identifying research related to specific topics:

> Has anyone come across some really good professional development materials and/or research related to helping older students? I would appreciate any resources you might suggest.

This request for help received eight responses, including the following one:

> I like to concur with other responders to your request that materials that are relevant to the purpose of why adults want to learn to read are highly beneficial to teaching them to read.

Some topics had great durability. Responses to a posting, for example, could occur over a span of months. One such topic was "Reading as an Art and Science," which received twenty-two responses over a period of four months. Another discussion thread, "Fluency," went on for nearly a year, with nineteen responses posted. This sort of interaction was common and thus topics were not archived, as the facilitator could not predetermine their possible duration.

Some members were consistently information providers. One frequent poster became known as the "Web resource provider" for posting Web resources in discussion threads and in shared documents. Web resources were in high demand, perhaps due to the limited time that members had for identifying such resources. The following is an example of a Web resource posting by a RFTEN member:

> For all those interested in reviewing an excellent ESL Website that offers an in-depth

understanding of cross-cultural language and academic development (CLAD) please see the following Website . . .

Those who posted resources were acknowledged and appreciated. The following is a response to the previous post:

> Hello . . . This Website is very useful. I will integrate this site in the reading courses that address diversity.

The same member who was appreciated for providing Web resources was identified as the "Documenter," taking pictures at the RFTEN professional development seminars and distributing them to members who provided a CD and mailer. Members appreciated the Documenter's commitment to the group, as evidenced by the following post:

> It was very thoughtful of you to take the initiative to capture and share a pictorial documentation of the July Collaborative Seminar. I will put the CD in the mail to you this week. Thank you for your generosity!

Faculty members also used the online community to recognize each other's achievements and offer congratulations and appreciation for contributions to the field, as in this post:

> Your presentation at IRA in the RFTEN Session was both interesting and informative. I was most interested in your assessment instruments. Please email me a copy of your handout and any other related information. Thanks in advance!

They also used the online community to provide support in difficult times. In the aftermath of Hurricane Katrina, members eagerly awaited information about the fate of their colleagues who had been in the path of the devastation. For them and many other regular HEC Online users who had been displaced, this online community was a way to stay connected. One member wrote,

> I am currently displaced from New Orleans, Louisiana, and working with Katrina's victims in shelters. I want everyone to know that having this Website is a lifesaver for me. My colleagues and I were able to access the resources, suggestions and information from this site. We were able to provide information to other colleagues who didn't know where to begin from a trusted source. Thanks to all of you. You have no idea how helpful you have been in all areas.

Because this was a threaded discussion, another user responded to this post by writing "Our hearts are with you! How can we help?"

Using HEC Online in the RFTEN Project:
Challenges and Lessons Learned

The challenge to participating fully in HEC Online most frequently cited by RFTEN participants was the lack of time. In an informal survey of twelve RFTEN faculty members, who were asked what they thought was the most difficult thing to do in terms of their *overall* RFTEN participation, six said it was "difficult to participate in HEC Online." Of those six, half attributed their difficulty to time constraints. RFTEN members cited the lack of access to appropriate and/or operational technology as the other significant challenge to full participation. For example, some members reported that they could participate in HEC Online only from their homes because they had access issues (outdated computers, security barriers that required intervention, and low bandwidth) when they tried to log in from their campus offices.

Technology support was provided for HEC Online, and documentation of that support, in the form of technical-support logs, was maintained. These logs documented some of what might be considered the temporary challenges to participation. The most frequently recorded temporary issues were forgotten passwords and forgotten or changed email addresses. Although such things as forgotten passwords should have been temporary setbacks or concerns, they often became long-term barriers. Too often members would simply stop using the online community until they attended an RFTEN professional development seminar where technical support staff or the facilitator could provide them with "on-the-spot" assistance. It was in these settings that members would report they had not used the community for months because they had experienced minor technical difficulties.

There were also members who simply did not find the online community to be of value to them. One such member stated that when she needed help, she immediately sought out colleagues at her institution. Another member stated that she preferred to talk directly with someone and did not care for electronic conversations where you could not see or hear the person with whom you were interacting.

For those considering launching a similar online community, I offer the following recommendations:

- Form focus groups made up of potential members of the community of users before building the community.
- Beta test the electronic environment with those users before widespread release.
- Gather together prospective users to discuss their needs and requirements from both a content and a navigational perspective (such discussions will

benefit the system's designers and prove beneficial to the participants in the long run if participants can avoid potential technical or navigational barriers that might hinder their successful use of and participation in the online community).

Although there may not be a great deal that can be done to address members' perceived lack of time for participating in HEC Online, perhaps more could be done to increase the "value added" perception of member participation in the online community discussions. Faculty members have to parse out their time across teaching, research, scholarship, service, and professional organization participation. To gain and enhance participation in the online community, faculty must be able to see its benefit as a resource for teaching and learning. In addition, participation and usage of HEC Online can be increased with institutional recognition and rewards. For example, institutions and unit heads can provide professional value and incentives for individual faculty when they recognize that HEC Online can be used for research, information sharing, and networking with experts in the field.

Summary

The value of participating in this online community appeared to be both professional and personal. RFTEN members requested and provided information. They communicated with one another around topics of concern to them. They supported one another's professional efforts and shared resources when needed. Members came to know and appreciate each other's contributions to the community and to the field of education. Some members participated fully, whereas others simply followed online interactions without participating. One member characterized her own participation as being merely an onlooker.

As the RFTEN grant drew to a close, members continued to post and to encourage one another to stay in touch. In the last month of the project, the member known as the "Documenter" wrote:

> We need to keep up the communication and friendships that we have built the last couple of years. Don't drop the ball because our commitment to RFTEN is about over. We need to keep the ball rolling for our students, our profession and ourselves.

CHAPTER FIVE

Reflections

RFTEN in Retrospect

CHARLES M. HODGE

Time will tell whether the objective of the RFTEN project—to improve the reading achievement level of elementary school students—was realized. The purpose of the project was to train a group of future teachers in new techniques and methodology for teaching reading on the basis of scientifically based reading research (SBRR). Engaging selected minority-serving institutions, the RFTEN project initiated a new approach to closing the achievement gap in reading. To that end, RFTEN is a worthy model for all students and for all schools. What follows is an overview of the RFTEN project and reflections on the genesis and expected outcome of the efforts supported by the U.S. Department of Education.

A Climate of Concern

In the climate of concern that existed when RFTEN began in 2003, reading was called the "new civil right." "You have to learn to read before you can read to learn" not only became a fitting tagline for the project but also described the urgency of addressing the achievement gap in reading. Research revealed that elementary school students were not mastering reading skills and that the lack of achievement disproportionately affected the minority student population. The failure of elementary students to master reading skills was threatening the educational process as a whole and damaging the future prospects of many students. The image and reputation of the nation's educational process were in jeopardy.

Over time, the problem was addressed in a variety of ways, resulting in limited improvement in the reading scores of students. Then, to add a new dimension to the issue, came the debate about phonics versus whole language as a methodological approach to improving reading scores. From the debate emerged methods that centered on new literature, different classroom teaching strategies, and renewed parental involvement in students' learning process to master reading skills. Yet reading scores for students in general and minority students in particular remained unacceptable. Thus, the RFTEN project was developed.

The RFTEN Approach

Born out of desperation, RFTEN represented the road not taken by other national efforts to improve reading scores. The RFTEN project worked to improve the technical and instructional skills of those charged with teaching reading skills in elementary schools. Because reading skills were disproportionately low among Black and other minority children, RFTEN focused its efforts on teacher preparation programs at selected minority-serving institutions. Historically Black Colleges and Universities comprised the majority of the participating RFTEN institutions. The project engaged teacher educators, training them in SBRR strategies that were modeled and taught to pre-service teachers. Institutional partners went a step further by seeking institutional commitments to the teaching of reading endorsed by presidents, deans, and other top administrators.

In fact, the president, provost, and dean from thirty-eight partner institutions agreed in writing to support efforts to improve the way teachers learned to teach reading. A group of reading experts provided by the RFTEN project was assigned to assist personnel in designing local strategies to improve reading instruction as a part of the teacher preparation program. The result was a variety of initiatives predicated on SBRR and instruction.

Although the RFTEN institutions were part of a collective, each institution was encouraged to implement RFTEN-based strategies suited to its institutions, community, and teacher candidates. All of the institutions, however, had a mandate from the project to engage and collaborate with local Reading First, hard-to-staff, or low-performing elementary schools. These partner schools provided places for teacher candidates to practice and use their new skills and SBRR instruction in the classroom. RFTEN succeeded in making the university, the classroom teacher, the community, and families part of the solution to the crisis in reading achievement.

Under the auspices of the RFTEN project, many teacher preparation programs were restructured to include additional reading courses. At other institutions the content of existing reading courses was realigned to include elements of SBRR. RFTEN provided institutions with materials and resources and with ongoing national instruction and networking opportunities (in person and online). Education faculty at RFTEN partner institutions participated in regular Collaborative Development Seminars as part of their professional development and were given opportunities to attend and present to national and international reading conferences.

University administrators, deans, provosts, and presidents proved to be catalysts in creating and sustaining change in the teacher preparation programs. It was through their efforts and engagement that their campuses recognized the impor tance of literacy and the need to promote reading as a major institutional initiative to be addressed at all administrative and academic levels. Throughout the project, RFTEN provided quality assurance coaching consultants and reading consultants to provide technical assistance and leadership and to support reading instruction, curriculum transformation, and coaching for faculty and administrators.

A Climate of Optimism for Ultimate Success

When RFTEN was implemented, the intended outcome was the restructuring of teacher preparation programs in reading instruction, with the ultimate goal of improving reading achievement among elementary students. RFTEN's efforts to transform reading curricula and launch university/school collaborations have made a difference in how children learn to read. The result has been increased reading scores among students taught by candidates enrolled in RFTEN/SBRR courses. In addition, many faculty and RFTEN institutions have successfully collaborated and engaged parents and community leaders in improving reading achievement using practical literacy skills and SBRR.

The design and delivery of the RFTEN project created a new paradigm for tackling the crisis in reading among young children. As new teachers emerge from RFTEN partner institutions prepared to excite and train children to read, we can only expect that improved reading skills and achievement will be realized. The ulti mate impact of the RFTEN project can be realized only if the work with the part ner institutions continues and if the programmatic model is given the opportunity and funding needed for it to be replicated at colleges, universities, and schools and in communities across the nation. Time will tell!

Afterword

PAULETTA BROWN BRACY

The ultimate goal of any educational enterprise is the assurance of student achievement. Reading to learn is fundamental to the assurance that students are successful and will achieve. Having teachers who are skilled with the ability to successfully teach children to learn to read and ultimately read to learn is the measure of accountability that assures the public that the teachers are highly qualified or prepared. Thus, teachers and administrators must assume responsibility for learning that is responsive to public demands and for satisfying the moral obligations to foster child development. And most importantly, the outcomes must be perceivable in the success of *any* student. It is the teacher who, as the pivotal player, initiates the process of learning but it is the "literate student" who becomes the true measure of accountability.

The preparation of the teacher is paramount and requires engagement in a process that can be characterized by commitment, compassion, competence, collaboration, coaching, and continuity.

Commitment to the profession—and, more significant, a moral commitment to the welfare of children—is an unequivocal requirements. Placing any child in a learning environment mandates the presumption or disposition that all children can learn. This premise should be a personal mantra for anyone in a classroom.

The landscape of education has changed, and student populations are more diverse than ever. Attention to cultural perspectives requires evolving sensitivity to styles of learning. *Compassion* is the element of caring and concern for children and for (personal) professionalism. This is an affective domain, and a keen sense of humanity must be clearly manifest for children in the behavior of teachers.

Teacher preparation programs include assessments which require evidence that education students are promising and viable teachers. Faculty and mandatory licensing examinations can attest that students "know" and "can do." Hence, content and pedagogy become foci for learning, and *competence* is affirmed.

The notion that learning is an individual experience is dispelled when one realizes that it is undoubtedly a result of teamwork. Teams of school educators are engaged in *collaboration*, extending the practice of teaching to connect with families and community agencies. To educate a child and guarantee academic success require outreach beyond the classroom.

The delivery of instruction in the classroom complemented by the process of learning is *coaching*. Education students learn how to teach content and then transfer these skills into the classroom to teach children. To facilitate learning and to affirm learning are the basis of this attribute. Teaching is incomplete unless assessment of learning is documented. With continuous improvement as a goal, as with any approach to assessment, the emphasis shifts from "input" to "output," and it is student performance that provides the results. And, if the results are unsatisfactory or unacceptable, teaching is modified to affect the outcome directly. The goal of success never changes; the strategy may and should if warranted.

The process is continuous. Successes should not be reported only quantitatively but qualitatively as well. Evidence of both types provides a more balanced perspective of a child's success. *Continuity* of best practices in teaching produces favorable results and is supported by canonical research which provides guidance for the profession and substantially advances student learning.

The observation of former Secretary of Education Roderick Paige—You cannot read to learn until you first learn to read—resonates throughout the case studies and project findings shared in this book. Rooted in scientifically based reading research (SBRR), the Reading First Teacher Education Network (RFTEN) can point to demonstrated results in the classroom. The project and findings offer viable models and practices that can be replicated. The project provides a framework for best practices and for students instructed in five components of reading—phonemic awareness, phonics, vocabulary, fluency, and reading comprehension—who can become proficient and adept readers. But strategies are meaningless unless they are documented with legitimate evidence. Essentially, the case studies inform the professional community of the lessons learned.

Extending Dr. Paige's vision to explore ways to close the achievement gap, and the foresight of Dr. Boyce C. Williams, RFTEN project director, to partner with selected Historically Black Colleges and Universities, Tribal Colleges and

Universities, and Hispanic-serving Institutions has given the RFTEN project national and global visibility and prominence. RFTEN's success, bolstered by the work and support of its partner institutions, makes it a model for the nation.

RFTEN Project Cohort 1 Participants

Alabama State University
Dr. Evelyn A. Hodge

Alcorn State University
Dr. Doris Gary
Ms. Delores G. Williams

Bethune-Cookman College
Dr. Estelle Brown

California State University, Northridge
Dr. Marilyn Joshua-Shearer

Coppin State University
Dr. Glynis Barber
Dr. Delores Harvey

Florida International University
Dr. Joyce Fine
Ms. Lynne Miller

Jackson State University
Dr. Ada Butler
Dr. Linda Channell

Langston University
Dr. Ruth Herts

Lincoln University
Dr. Cheryl Hibbett

Livingstone College
Dr. Kellee Dillard Watkins

Morgan State University
Dr. Patricia Welch

Oakwood College
Dr. Frances Bliss

Oglala Lakota College
Mr. Tom Raymond

South Dakota State University
Dr. Susan McWilliams

Virginia State University
Ms. Donna Miles Jones

Xavier University of Louisiana
Dr. Rosalind Green

RFTEN Project Cohort 2 Participants

Alabama State University
Dr. Danjuma Saulawa
Dr. Franklin Witherspoon

Albany State University
Dr. Audrey Beard
Dr. Patricia Jenkins

Alcorn State University
Dr. Orlenthea McGowan
Dr. Tracy Neal

Bethune-Cookman College
Dr. Vera Lenning

California State University, Fullerton
Dr. Beth Schipper

California State University, Northridge
Dr. Shammy Bogosian

Dr. Margaret Espinosa-Nelson
Dr. Nancy Prosenjak

Coppin State University
Dr. Juanita Ashby-Bey
Dr. Leontye Lewis
Dr. Kathy Grant

Florida International University
Dr. Lisbeth Dixon-Krauss
Dr. Nancy Marshall
Dr. Joyce Fine
Ms. Lynne Miller

Hampton University
Dr. Elsie Daniels
Dr. Judith Brooks-Buck

Jackson State University
Dr. Virgia D. Gambrell

Kean University
Dr. Joan Kastner
Dr. Ethel Young

Langston University
Dr. Sharlene Johnson
Dr. Emily L. Porter

Lincoln University
Dr. Avila Hendricks
Dr. Sharon Shockley Lee

Livingstone College
Mrs. Cora Hill

Morgan State University
Dr. Solomon Alao
Dr. Virginia C. Johns

Norfolk State University
Dr. Matilda Martin
Dr. Carol Rhodes J. Nelson
Dr. Arletha McSwain

North Carolina A&T State University
Dr. David Boger
Dr. Elizabeth J. Davis-Seaver

North Carolina Central University
Dr. Ioney James
Dr. Joy Banks
Dr. Yolanda Dunston

Oakwood College
Dr. Artie Melancon
Ms. Marilyn Schenck

Oglala Lakota College
Ms. Shannon Amiotte
Ms. Terri Bissonette

South Dakota State University
Dr. Loye Romereim-Holmes
Dr. Lynda Venhuizen

Southern University at Baton Rouge
Dr. Eva B. Kleinpeter
Dr. Bobbie Robertson

Southern University at New Orleans
Dr. Melba Venison
Dr. Ana Lamikanra
Dr. Rita Ann Mitchell

Tennessee State University
Dr. Jill Speering
Dr. Beth Quick

University of Arkansas at Pine Bluff
Dr. Linda Joshua

University of Maryland Eastern Shore
Dr. Mary L. Agnew

Virginia State University
Dr. Delores R. Greene
Ms. Donna Jones-Miles
Dr. Judaea Hodge
Dr. Carolyn H. Wilson

Virginia Union University
Dr. William F. Johnson, Jr.
Dr. Wilbert Jenkins

Xavier University of Louisiana
Dr. Deborah E. Bordelon
Dr. Tanzia Prosper

York College of New York
Dr. Lindamichelle Baron
Dr. Wynne A. Shilling

RFTEN Project Cohort 3 Participants

Alabama State University
Mrs. Parichart Thornton

Central State University
Dr. Hazel Latson

Cheney University of Pennsylvania
Ms. Cynthia Tuleja

Delaware State University
Dr. Suzanne Iovino
Dr. Joseph Falodun

Hampton University
Dr. Letizia Gambrell-Boone
Dr. Gertrude Henry
Dr. Elsie Daniels

Haskell Indian Nations University
Ms. Jackie Boyd
Ms. Kay McCord

Kean University
Dr. Davida Schuman
Dr. Deborah Allen

Morgan State University
Dr. Evon Jackson
Dr. Virginia C. Johns

Paine College
Ms. Debbie MacDonald
Ms. Floydena Walker

New Mexico Highlands University
Dr. James Abreu
Dr. Nicole Montague

Saint Paul's College
Mrs. Emma Staples

Stillman College
Dr. Estelle Ryan Clavelli
Dr. Sandra J. Jemison

Southern University at New Orleans
Dr. Melba Venison
Dr. Rita Ann Mitchell

Tennessee State University
Dr. Beth N. Quick
Dr. Beth Christian

Virginia State University
Dr. Judith Brooks-Buck

West Virginia State University
Dr. Robert L. Harrison, Jr.
Ms. Jenny Mayo

Winston-Salem State University
Dr. Cassaundra El-Amin
Dr. Kathy Grant

York College-CUNY
Dr. Veronica Shipp

RFTEN Institutional Participants

Deans and Department Chairs

Alabama
Dr. Gwendolyn Trotter, Dean
College of Education
Alabama State University

Dr. James Mbyirukira, Coordinator
Department of Education
Oakwood College

Dr. Linda Bradford, Dean
College of Education
Stillman College

Arkansas
Dr. Calvin Johnson, Dean
School of Education
University of Arkansas at Pine Bluff

Delaware
Dr. Doris E. Wooledge, Dean
College of Education & Sport Sciences
Delaware State University

Florida
Dr. Lorraine Daniels-Day,
    Former Dean
School of Education
Bethune-Cookman College

Georgia
Dr. Wilburn Campbell, Dean
College of Education
Albany State University

Dr. Francesina R. Jackson,
    Department Chair
Division of Education
Paine College

146 | APPENDIX 4

Louisiana
Dr. Gussie Trahan, Interim Dean
College of Education
Southern University at Baton Rouge

Dr. Rose Duhon-Sells, Dean
College of Education
Southern University at New Orleans

Dr. Deborah Bordelon, (Former
    Dept. Chair)
Department of Education
Xavier University of Louisiana

Maryland
Dr. Julius Chapman, Dean
Department of Education
Coppin State University

Dr. Patricia Welch, Dean
School of Education & Urban Studies
Morgan State University

Dr. Karen Verbeke, Department Chair
Department of Education
University of Maryland, Eastern Shore

Mississippi
Dr. Josephine Posey, Dean
School of Education
Alcorn State University

Dr. Ivory Phillips, Dean
School of Education & Human
    Development
Jackson State University

Missouri
Dr. Patrick Henry, Dean
College of Liberal Arts,

Education & Journalism
Lincoln University

North Carolina
Dr. Leroy Simmons, Dean
School of Education & Social Work
Livingstone College

Dr. Lelia Vickers, Dean
School of Education
North Carolina A&T State University

Dr. Cecelia Steppe-Jones, Dean
School of Education
North Carolina Central University

Dr. Cynthia Jackson-Hammond, Dean
Department of Education
Winston-Salem State University

Ohio
Dr. Kaye Manson Jeter, Dean
College of Education
Central State University

Oklahoma
Dr. Darnell Williams, Dean
College of Education & Behavioral
    Sciences
Langston University

Pennsylvania
Dr. Cathine G. Gilchrist, Dean
College of Education
Cheney University of Pennsylvania

South Dakota
Dr. Laurie Nichols, (Former Dean)
College of Family & Consumer Science
South Dakota State University

Dr. Hank Rubin, (Former Co-Dean)
College of Family & Consumer Science
South Dakota State University

Mr. Art Fisher, Dean
College of Education
Oglala Lakota College

Tennessee
Dr. Leslie Drummond, Associate Dean
College of Education
Tennessee State University

Virginia
Dr. Mamie Locke, Dean
School of Liberal Arts & Education
Hampton University

Dr. Jean Braxton, Dean
School of Education
Norfolk State University

Dr. W. Weldon Hill, Dean
School of Liberal Arts & Education
Virginia State University

Dr. Joy Goodrich, Dean
School of Education &
Interdisciplinary Studies
Virginia Union University

West Virginia
Dr. Robert L. Harrison, Jr.
Department of Education
West Virginia State University

RFTEN President's Advisory Council

Council Member

Dr. Judith Albino, Alliant International University (CA)

Dr. Belinda Anderson, Virginia Union University

Dr. Delbert W. Baker, Oakwood College (AL)

Dr. Lionel Bordeaux, Sinte Gleska University (SD)

Dr. Clinton Bristow, Jr., Alcorn State University (MS)

Dr. Lawrence Davis, Jr., University of Arkansas, Pine Bluff

Dr. Norman Francis (Chair), Xavier University of Louisiana

Dr. Algeania Freeman, Livingstone College (NC)

Dr. Peggy Gordon-Miller, South Dakota State University

Dr. William Harvey/ Dr. JoAnn W. Haysbert, Hampton University (VA)

Dr. James Heffner, Tennessee State University

Dr. David B. Henson, Lincoln University (MO)

Dr. Ernest L. Holloway, Langston University (OK)

Dr. Edward Jackson, Southern University, Baton Rouge

Dr. Jolene Koester, California State University, Northridge

Dr. Joe E. Lee, Alabama State University

Dr. Ronald Mason, Jr., Jackson State University (MS)

Dr. Marie McDemmond, Norfolk State University (VA)

Dr. James Renick, North Carolina A&T State University
Dr. Earl S. Richardson, Morgan State University (MD)
Dr. Press Robinson, Southern University, New Orleans
Dr. Portia H. Shields, Albany State University (GA)
Dr. Thomas Shortbull, Oglala Lakota (SD)

Contributors

RoSusan D. Bartee, Ph.D., is an associate professor of Educational Leadership at the University of Mississippi in Oxford, Mississippi. Dr. Bartee's research interests are K-12 education leadership, social contexts of schools, and university-school partnerships. Dr. Bartee teaches educational leadership, research methods, and cultural contexts of education courses. Previously, she was the Associate Project Director for the National Council for Accreditation of Teacher Education/Reading First Teacher Education Network (NCATE/RFTEN) and Interim Executive Director at the Frederick D. Patterson Research Institute of the United Negro College Fund (UNCF). Dr. Bartee holds a Bachelor of Arts degree from Tougaloo College in Mississippi. She received her Master of Arts from Northwestern University in Illinois and Doctorate of Philosophy from the University of Illinois at Urbana-Champaign.

Pauletta Brown Bracy, Ph.D., is associate professor of Library and Information Sciences at North Carolina Central University where she teaches courses in youth services and school media librarianship. Dr. Bracy is also Director of University Accreditation at North Carolina Central University. She served as a Quality Assurance Coaching Consultant for the Reading First Teacher Education Network (RFTEN) project and is a national expert on ethnic materials for children and young adults.

Her work with the National Council for Accreditation of Teacher Education (NCATE) has included serving as a Board of Examiners member and as a member and chair on NCATE's Specialty Areas Studies Board and its Executive Board. She is an active member and leader of The American Library Association. She is a graduate of Fisk University, the University of Michigan, and the University of Iowa.

M. Christopher Brown II, Ph.D., is professor and dean of the College of Education at the University of Nevada, Las Vegas. He previously served as Vice President for Programs and Administration at the American Association of Colleges for Teacher Education, Director of Social Justice and Professional Development for the American Educational Research Association, as well as former Executive Director and Chief Research Scientist of the Frederick D. Patterson Research Institute of the United Negro College Fund.

Dr. Brown has written and edited twelve books and monographs including: *Achieving Equitable Educational Outcomes with All Students* (2005), *The Children Hurricane Katrina Left Behind* (2007), *School Matters* (2007), and *Still Not Equal* (2007); and has lectured on six continents. He received his Ph.D. in Higher Education from The Pennsylvania State University.

Brian Bryant, Ph.D., lives and works in Austin, Texas, where he moved after teaching special education public school students for three years in Maine. He has served in many professional capacities, including director of research at Pro-Ed, Inc., adjunct faculty member at the University of Texas at Austin, and Research Fellow at the University of Texas Vaughn Gross Center for Reading and Language Arts. Dr. Bryant has been a visiting professor at several colleges across the country and has worked as a consultant on numerous projects, including RFTEN and the University of Texas System's TRAKS Project. He is the author of more than 100 articles, tests, professional development guides, and books/chapters in books. Dr. Bryant's research interests include service provision for individuals with learning disabilities and mental retardation, particularly with regard to reading, mathematics, and assistive technology applications throughout the lifespan.

Lecretia A. Buckley, Ph.D., is an assistant professor of mathematics education in the Department of Curriculum and Instruction in the College of Education at Purdue University. Dr. Buckley's research interests include equity issues in mathematics education. In her research, she examines preservice and in-service secondary mathematics teachers' conceptions of equity. Dr. Buckley was an external evaluator for the RFTEN program.

Linda Colburn, Ph.D., is a statewide Reading First coordinator and project director at the Vaughn Gross Center for Reading and Language Arts at the University of Texas at Austin. She was previously an assistant clinical professor of technology and education at Vanderbilt University in Nashville, Tennessee, where she was actively involved in the preparation of teachers. She has developed and taught courses for graduate and undergraduate students in the areas of early reading, children's literature, technology integration, cognition and technology, and curriculum design and instructional and assistive technology. She has published in many journals and coauthored several book chapters on topics ranging from anchoring instruction to supporting teacher change. Dr. Colburn has also worked as a consultant, supporting RFTEN faculty through site visits.

Emerson J. Elliott, in 1995, after over thirty years and seven presidential administrations, retired from the U.S. Department of Education as Director of The National Center for Education Statistics. Previously Mr. Elliott directed and headed offices in the Department of Health, Education and Welfare, and the Office of Management and Budget (OMB). Mr. Elliott has received Presidential Rank Awards for Meritorious and Distinguished Performance, the Education Leadership Award of the Council on American Private Education, and was elected an American Statistical Association Fellow in 1996. Currently he works as Director of Special Projects for the National Council for Accreditation of Teacher Education and served as Director of Evaluation for the Reading First Teacher Education Network (RFTEN) grant project. He is a graduate of Albion College and the University of Michigan.

Joyce C. Fine, Ed. D., is an associate professor for Reading/ Language Arts in the College of Education at Florida International University in the Department of Curriculum and Instruction. Dr. Fine is the Program Leader in Reading at Florida International University. She served as the Reading First Teacher Education Network (RFTEN) representative at the University.

B. Denise Hawkins, M.A., an award-winning journalist, served as RFTEN's communications director and writer. Ms. Hawkins is a contributing writer for *Diverse: Issues in Higher Education* magazine and for *Howard University Magazine.* Her stories have also been published in the *Washington Post*, Religion News Service, *Black Issues in Higher Education, Today's Christian*, and *Christian Reader.* She earned her M.A. from The Pennsylvania State University and her B.A. from Howard University. Ms. Hawkins was a writer and editorial consultant for the book *Reforming Teacher Education through Accreditation: Telling Our Story*, published by the National Council for Accreditation of Teacher Education in 2000.

Charles M. Hodge, Ed.D., who recently retired and lives in Jacksonville, Florida, is the former associate provost and dean of the Graduate School at Bowie State University, Maryland. He was also dean of the College of Education at Western Michigan University, Lamar University (Texas), and the University of Central Arkansas and was on the staff of the higher education coordinating board in both Texas and Arkansas. Currently, Dr. Hodge is a quality assurance consultant with the RFTEN project. His work on educators for a democratic system of schooling is included in the book, *Access to Knowledge*, published by the College Board and edited by John Goodlad and Pam Keating.

Denise Littleton, Ed.D., is a professor in the Department of Early Childhood/Elementary Education at Norfolk State University in Norfolk, Virginia. Dr. Littleton was a public school teacher in Indiana and Pennsylvania, a reading clinician at George Washington University, and a research associate at the U.S. Department of Education in the former Department of Special Education and Rehabilitative Services. Dr. Littleton has authored and directed grants totaling more than two million dollars from private and federal sources. She served as a consultant for the RFTEN grant project. Dr. Littleton's presentations, published articles, and research interests focus on issues related to teacher preparation, reading, and urban/multicultural education.

Diana W. Rigden, Ph.D., is vice president of the Teacher Education Accreditation Council. She came to TEAC from the American Association of Colleges for Teacher Education (AACTE), where she was a senior associate. From 2000 to 2004, Rigden was vice president and director of the Higher Education Program, and from 1995–2000 directed the Teacher Education Program at the Council for Basic Education. Before this, she was vice president of Precollege Programs for the Council for Aid to Education in New York.

John Taylor, Ed.D., earned his master's and doctoral degrees from Stanford University, Palo Alto, California, in 1976. Before entering Stanford, he taught at Menlo Atherton High School, Merritt Community College, and the University of San Francisco. From 1976 through 1989, he was an assistant professor at the University of Illinois, Urbana-Champaign, and associate, senior associate, and director of the Learning and Instruction Division of the Office of Educational Research and Improvement (OERI) in the U.S. Department of Education. Dr. Taylor was dean and professor of the College of Education at California State University, Chico (1989 to 1991) and dean and professor of the College of Education at the University of Arizona (1991 to 2002). Currently, he is a graduate professor of educational leadership. His current research and scholarship focus on educational policy, leadership, and program evaluation. He was an external evaluator of the RFTEN site visits.

Margaret Cole White, Ed.D., is currently Director of Teacher Education at Elizabeth City State University in Elizabeth City, North Carolina. She served as a Quality Assurance Coaching Consultant for the Reading First Teacher Education Network (RFTEN) project. Dr. White has also served as a Board of Examiners member for the National Council for Accreditation of Teacher Education (NCATE). She is a graduate of Hampton University and East Carolina University and received her doctorate from Virginia Polytechnic Institute and State University.

Boyce C. Williams, Ph.D., is an educator and a visionary. As vice president at the National Council for Accreditation of Teacher Education (NCATE), Dr. Williams works closely with institutions to help implement the accreditation process smoothly and efficiently. Dr. Williams served as project director of the Historically Black Colleges and Universities Technical Support Network, as well as project director for the NCATE/National Board for Professional Teaching Standards Partnership for Graduate Programs. She was project director of a $4.5 million dollar grant from the U.S. Department of Education for RFTEN. Dr. Williams served as editor of *Reforming Teacher Education through Accreditation: Telling Our Story*. She has authored numerous articles and monographs on issues related to quality teacher preparation and student learning. In addition to receiving four honorary Doctorate Degrees, she earned her Bachelor of Arts degree from The Lincoln University in Pennsylvania and her Master of Arts and Doctorate of Philosophy from Michigan State University.

Arthur E. Wise, Ph.D., is president of the National Council for Accreditation of Teacher Education (NCATE). During his career, Dr. Wise has worked toward teacher quality and professionalism, school finance reform, and the advancement of educational research.

Dr. Wise is co-author of *A License to Teach*, which is a blueprint for the professionalization of teaching. In 1968 he authored *Rich Schools, Poor Schools: The Promise of Equal Educational Opportunity* and in 1979 *Legislated Learning*. Dr. Wise was associate director for research, National Institute of Education, Department of Education and Welfare. Subsequently, at the Office of Management and Budget, he helped to create the separate cabinet-level U. S. Department of Education. Dr. Wise received a Bachelors Degree from Harvard College and his MBA and Ph.D. from The University of Chicago.

Reflections

It took vision and courage to launch and implement the Reading First Teacher Education Network (RFTEN) in 2003. The goals of this pilot project were ambitious, and its funding was modest by federal standards. From the outset, RFTEN did not waste time trying to enter through the periphery of a national crisis—the disparity in reading achievement. Instead, RFTEN dove in through the middle to fuel and support a transformation in teacher education through partnerships with nearly forty Historically Black Colleges and Universities, Tribal Colleges, and Hispanic-serving Institutions and the U.S. Department of Education. Using a top-down approach that engaged college and university presidents and other senior administrators, and by training teacher educators, RFTEN has succeeded in equipping teacher candidates with effective and scientifically based reading strategies they can use when they enter the classroom. But, most important, RFTEN, through its network of dedicated reading experts, candidates, faculty, deans, and presidents, is demonstrating that scientifically based reading research is a strategy that can make a profound difference in the lives of struggling and minority readers.

As we know from reform in the K–12 system and mounting discussions on accountability and teacher quality, it comes down to what happens with instruction, what happens in that classroom. It is very difficult to have an impact there, but RFTEN has demonstrably been able to do just this through its partner institutions and the higher education/public school collaborations that have been forged during the project. In the area of reading, there is more than three decades of solid research on which to build and on which to draw. RFTEN ventured forth and tapped into this reservoir of reading knowledge and strategies to ensure that teacher candidates have access to the information that comes out of such research.

Michael J. Petrilli is vice president for national programs and policy at the Thomas B. Fordham Foundation, a Washington-based school reform organization. He served as a Bush administration appointee in the U.S. Department of Education (2001–2005), where he helped coordinate No Child Left Behind's public school choice and supplemental services provisions and oversaw discretionary grant programs for charter schools, alternative teacher certification, and high school reform. His work has appeared in *The New York Times, The Wall Street Journal, Education Next, Education Week, The Public Interest,* and other venues. He holds a B.A. in political science and a teaching certificate in secondary social studies from the University of Michigan.

In memory of Dr. Clinton Bristow Jr.
(March 19, 1949 to August 19, 2006),
the sixteenth president of Alcorn State University,
was a presidential leader in the Reading First Teacher Education Network